A Revolutionary War Road Trip on US Route 9

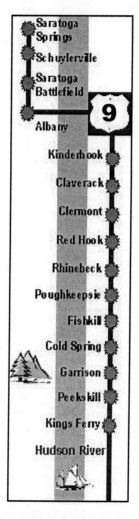

**Spend a Revolutionary Day Along
One of America's Most Historic Routes**

OTHER REVOLUTIONARY WAR ROAD TRIPS
By Raymond C. Houghton

A Revolutionary War Road Trip on US Route 9

Spend a Revolutionary Day Along
One of America's Most Historic Routes

Raymond C. Houghton

Cyber Haus
Delmar, NY

A Revolutionary War Road Trip on US Route 9
Spend a Revolutionary Day Along
One of America's Most Historic Routes

Revolutionary War Road Trips
are published by Cyber Haus
and printed on-demand
by Booksurge, LLC,
www.booksurge.com,
1-866-308-6235.

ISBN: 1-931373-12-4

Cyber Haus
159 Delaware Avenue, #145
Delmar, NY 12054
www.revolutionaryday.com
www.cyhaus.com
cyhaus@msn.com
518-478-9798

To H. Russell Denegar
in gratitude for
his friendship
and support.

INTRODUCTION

US Route 9 goes from Maryland to Canada, but along the Hudson River, Route 9 goes through many cities and towns that played an important role in the American Revolution. During the time of the Revolution, the Hudson River was both a major transportation route and a geographic barrier. British control of the Hudson River as well as Lake Champlain would not only divide the American colonies but it would also cut communication and eliminate a very navigable passage as an American transportation route. At the same time for the British, it would open a major supply route from New Britain (Canada) to New York City, which were both held by the British for most of war.

In the spring of 1777, British General Burgoyne planned a three-pronged invasion to divide the colonies along the Champlain and Hudson valleys. The invasion would come from Canada in the north, New York City in the south and Lake Ontario in the west. The target for all three was Albany, NY.

Unfortunately for Burgoyne, his invasion from the north stalled at Saratoga (Stillwater, NY) and the invasion from the west stalled at Fort Stanwix (Rome, NY). The invasion from the south was never agreed to by General William Howe, who commanded the forces in New York City. Instead, he

John Burgoyne

By S.Hollyer

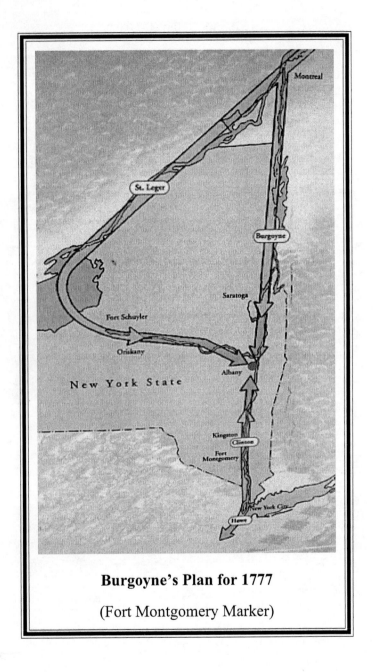

Burgoyne's Plan for 1777

(Fort Montgomery Marker)

decided to launch an invasion up Chesapeake Bay to Philadelphia. However, Howe left the decision to move north up to General Henry Clinton, who was left in charge of the forces in New York City. His instructions were for Clinton to make a move to Albany, "if the circumstances warranted."

Clinton's primary mission was to defend New York City, but he was also very cautious. He would not send troops northward unless he felt he had enough manpower to carry out both his defense of New York and an attack on Albany. Finally, in October of 1777, he decided to mount a "distraction" to the north but he did not intended to target Albany or rescue Burgoyne.

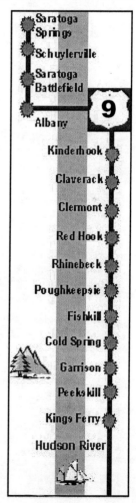

Clinton easily moved northward up the Hudson and took the Highland Passes north of Peekskill. He also sent an advance unit under the command of Major General John Vaughan to attack areas above the Highlands, including Kingston and Clermont. None of these areas were well defended because Washington had most of the American forces near Philadelphia and Saratoga. But when General Israel Putnam, who was shadowing the northward advance, got close enough to threaten the invasion, the British forces returned to

New York City. It is ironic that the most successful of the three prongs had a quick, very successful advance, but was started too late and was cautiously suspended when threatened.

A Revolutionary War Road Trip on US Route 9 begins early in the morning at Kings Ferry. During the Revolutionary War, Kings Ferry was a major crossing point on the Hudson. Because the British controlled New York City, Kings Ferry was the southernmost crossing point for American personnel and supplies for most of the war.

From Kings Ferry, the road trip heads north through Peekskill, Garrison and Cold Spring to Fishkill, which was the site of a large supply depot for the northern department of the Continental Army.

From Fishkill, the road trip continues north through Poughkeepsie, Rhinebeck and Red Hook to Clermont, which was the furthest north Clinton's 1777 invasion from New York City reached.

From Clermont, the road trip continues north through Claverack and Kinderhook, where Burgoyne would be briefly kept as a prisoner/ guest.

From Kinderhook, the road trip crosses the Hudson River to Albany, which was the target for the British invasions of 1777.

From Albany, the road trip continues north to the Saratoga Battlefield, where Burgoyne's invasion from the north would be stopped.

From Saratoga, the road trip continues north to Schuylerville, where Burgoyne surrendered, and then from Schuylerville, the road trip concludes in Saratoga Springs.

So, if you're ready, begin your **Revolutionary Day** along historic US Route 9.

TABLE OF CONTENTS
AND
TRIP LOG

Kings Ferry, New York: Kings Ferry was the southernmost crossing point on the Hudson for American personnel and supplies for most of the Revolutionary War. It was also a British target.

Kings Ferry to Peekskill: Travel past the Post Hannock House where in 1782 Washington presented medals to the captors of General Clinton's Adjutant General, Major André.

Peekskill, New York: Washington set up camp in Peekskill in 1781 and waited for French forces under the command of General Rochambeau.

Peekskill to Garrison: Climb the Highlands for a view of the Hudson and the former location of Fort Clinton and Fort Montgomery.

Garrison, New York: Walk to a pagoda on the Hudson where you get a great view of the United States Military Academy at West Point and the former location of Fort Arnold.

Rhinebeck, New York: Visit Beekman Arms, the oldest, still active tavern in America. In operation since 1766, it was visited by George Washington in 1775.

Rhinebeck to Red Hook: Pass by the original location of the Village of Rhinebeck and site of the oldest church in the northern precinct of Dutchess County.

Red Hook, New York: Visit a town that has been extending its hospitality to travelers for over 200 years.

Red Hook to Clermont: Travel west to the banks of the Hudson River and the most northern area reached by the British invasion from New York City in 1777.

Clermont, New York: Visit the home of the Livingston family, including Robert R. Livingston who was a member of the Continental Congress and the committee of five that drafted the Declaration of Independence.

Clermont to Livingston: Pass by the old Clermont Inn, which, in its day, was a prominent inn on the Albany-New York Post Road.

Saratoga Springs, New York: Visit the High Rock Spring, the former home of American spy, Alexander Bryan and a place visited by Philip Schuyler, George Washington, Alexander Hamilton and Governor Clinton of New York.

Kings Ferry

During the Revolution this vital crossing was located here. Used by French and American armies on march to Yorktown in 1781.

Cortlandt Historical Society, 1999

(Verplanck Marker)

KINGS FERRY, NEW YORK

Kings Ferry was a major crossing point on the Hudson. It connected Verplanck's Point on the east side of the Hudson with Stony Point on the west side. Since the British controlled New York City for most of the war, Kings Ferry was the southernmost crossing point for American personnel and supplies for most of the war. It was also a very important communication line between the north and the south. Therefore, Kings Ferry was a very strategic target for the British.

On October 5, 1777, Clinton dispersed the American forces at Verplanck's Point and landed 3,000 troops to secure the area for an attack up river. On October 6th, they took Stony Point across the river and then moved north to take Fort Clinton, Fort Montgomery and Constitution Island.

On October 8, 1777, George Washington sent a letter to William Livingston. "Sir: I yesterday received certain intelligence, that the enemy had proceeded up Hudson's River from New York, and landed a body of men at Verplanck's Point, a few miles below Peekskill. … Should any disaster happen, it is easy to foresee the most unhappy consequences. The loss of the Highland passes would be likely to involve the reduction of the forts. This would open the navigation of the river, and enable the enemy, with facility, to throw their force into Albany, get into the rear of General Gates, and either oblige him to retreat, or put him between two fires."

On May 30, 1779, the British returned to Kings Ferry. Six thousand troops left New York City by land and water, and moved across to Stony Point. On June 1st, while 40 American soldiers were finishing a blockhouse at Stony Point, the first British ships appeared in Haverstraw Bay. The soldiers burned the blockhouse and fled.

On June 1st, British forces attacked 70 North Carolina troops stationed at Fort Lafayette at Verplanck's Point. The American troops surrendered cutting off the important east-west link at King's Ferry. Also, the victories put the British in control of the gateway to the Hudson, just 12 miles south of West Point.

On the night of July 15-16, 1779, Brigadier General Anthony Wayne of Pennsylvania led the American Light Infantry in a daring midnight assault against the British forces at Stony Point. Two American columns

The American Strategy at Stony Point

In reaction to Sir Henry Clinton's move against Stony Point, the Continental Army marched north from New Jersey, to protect West Point, and a plan was devised to counter the British advance.

Apprised of the formidable British defenses at Stony Point by Captain Allan McLane, an American officer who had gained entrance to the enemy fort, General Washington determined that a frontal attack in daylight would most likely fail. Consequently, a night assault, to be led by Brigadier General Anthony Wayne of Pennsylvania, was planned.

Wayne commanded the Corps of Light Infantry, a select force which probed enemy lines, fought skirmishes and executed difficult missions. Two columns — a total of 1150 men — would comprise the Continental force. The main assault group of 700 men, commanded personally by General Wayne, would wade through the waters on the southern flank. At the same time, a smaller secondary column would approach from the north. To eliminate the possibility of accidental gunfire and preserve the key element of surprise, both columns were armed with unloaded muskets and fixed bayonets. In the center of the peninsula, two companies of North Carolina troops, commanded by Major Hardy Muffee, would fire volleys to distract the British and divert the fort's defenders. An additional force of 300 men, under General Peter Muhlenberg of Pennsylvania, would be held in reserve. At midnight, July 15, 1779, the attack would begin.

(Stony Point Marker)

outflanked the front line defenses and captured the garrison. The main assault column waded through the shallow waters of Haverstraw Bay, south of Stony Point. The secondary column approached around the north side of the Peninsula. The American victory at Stony Point was the last major battle in the north.

After the battle, the Americans destroyed the fort, removed the prisoners and captured supplies and equipment, including 16 pieces of artillery. Two days later, General Washington abandoned the peninsula, having determined that it could not be defended against the combined might of the British army and navy.

When the Americans withdrew, the British returned, and built a second fort with blockhouses surrounded by an abatis, but the war continued to expand. Crown forces were fighting the French and the Spanish, now allied with the Americans. With the additional burden on military resources and the decision to move the war to the American south as well as a lack of reinforcements, the British were compelled to abandon the forts at Stony Point and Verplanck's Point in October 1779. Kings Ferry was once again the southernmost crossing point on the Hudson.

Count de Rochambeau

by J. D. Court

In August 1781, Washington made the pivotal decision of the American Revolution. He decided to abandon operations in New York, sneak across the Hudson at Kings Ferry with French troops under the command of General Rochambeau and immediately march to the south to surprise Cornwallis at Yorktown. The American victory at Yorktown was the last major battle of the American Revolution.

In the summer of 1782, the Continental Army took to the field for the last time at Verplanck's Point. In a show of strength, the combined armies of General Washington and General Rochambeau demonstrated their might to the British bottled-up in New York City. The combined forces totaled 12,000.

The defeat at Yorktown, the assistance of the French and a war that had become unpopular in England forced the British to the peace table. Congress ratified the peace treaty on April 15, 1783 and the British evacuated New York City on November 25, 1783.

Today, a marker and a small park are at the spot where Kings Ferry leaves Verplanck's Point. Across the Hudson, is the Stony Point Battlefield. On a clear day, you can see the lighthouse at Stony Point.

Lighthouse at Stony Point

KINGS FERRY TO PEEKSKILL

Mile Mark 0.0 — The Kings Ferry crossing is at Verplanck's Point, which is at the intersection of Riverview and Broadway in the town of Verplanck. Begin your **Revolutionary Day** by taking Broadway to the center of town.

Mile Mark 0.2 — Pass the Broadway Restaurant on the right.

Mile Mark 0.3 — Reach the light at the intersection with 6th Street. Turn right and proceed up 6th Street, which becomes Kings Ferry Road. Pass the Trail's End Deli on the left and C&R Deli and Pizza on the right.

Mile Mark 0.7 — 6th Street becomes Kings Ferry Road. Watch for the original Kings Ferry crossing marker on the right and the Post Hannock House on the left.

Kings Ferry

This was the original site of this river crossing used in colonial days. Moved during the Revolution to the area of Fort Lafayette.

Cortlandt Historical Society 1999

(Kings Highway Marker)

24

As the marker in front of the Hannock House indicates, this is where George Washington presented medals to the captors of Major John André, Clinton's adjutant general. André was captured on September 20, 1780 attempting to pass between British and American lines in order to return to New York City after meeting with Benedict Arnold. Arnold was the commander of West Point and he wanted to complete final plans for his treasonous sale of West Point to the British.

When Arnold heard about the capture of André, he commandeered a barge and its crew. Leaving his wife and child behind, he ordered them to row him out to the British ship, "the Vulture," which was anchored out of range of West Point artillery.

Arnold escaped, joined the enemy and led British forces against Americans in Virginia and Connecticut

25

Kennedy House

Stood on this site. In 1777 Alexander Hamilton lay ill here for 2 weeks. The court martial that tried General Lee met here July 15, 1778.

Cortlandt Historical
Society 1999

(Kings Highway Marker)

before hostilities would subside after Yorktown. Thus, the name, Benedict Arnold, and the name, traitor, would become synonymous. However, this Benedict Arnold is a very different Benedict Arnold than the one we will meet at the end of this **Revolutionary Day**.

Mile Mark 1.1 — Look for the Kennedy House Marker that is in front of the library. Alexander Hamilton recuperated from illness here. Also, General Charles Lee was removed from command here. General Lee might have been able to end the American Revolution three years earlier if he had carried out Washington's orders. He chose not to attack the vulnerable British army after they had abandoned Philadelphia to return to New York City in June of 1778.

Mile Mark 1.3 — Reach one of a couple lights on Kings Ferry Road that seems to be placed at intersections that shouldn't need one. Bear right at this light.

Mile Mark 1.6 — Reach the second light. Bear left at this one.

Mile Mark 1.9 — Reach the intersection with Route 9A in the town of Cortlandt. This road was the old Albany to New York Post Road. The road was established in 1772 and provided weekly mail service and covered wagon, passenger service in the mid 1780's.

Turn left, heading north on Route 9A.

Mile Mark 2.1 — Pass Hendrick Hudson High School on the left.

Mile Mark 3.1 — Reach the Westchester Diner on the left. This classic diner is a good place to catch a quick breakfast.

From the diner, continue north for a short distance on US Route 9A. Get into the left lane as you approach the light before the US Route 9 bridge. At the light, turn right and get into the middle lane so you can make the left turn onto US Route 9 heading north.

Mile Mark 4.2 — Take the exit to Hudson Avenue in Peekskill. At the stop sign, turn left onto Hudson Avenue and cross the railroad tracks and enter the park on the Hudson River.

Mile Mark 4.5 — Arrive in Peekskill.

PEEKSKILL

On March 23, 1777, 500 British troops disembarked from 10 ships sent up the Hudson to attack the storehouse at Peekskill. 250 American troops manned the storehouse at Peekskill under the command of Alexander McDougall. McDougall withdrew into the town and asked for support from Fort Montgomery across the river. Col Marinus Willett arrived with 80 men and with the General's permission led an attack on the British who were burning military supplies. Willett fired on the British and charged with bayonets forcing the British to retreat.

Four years later, Washington set up camp in Peekskill and waited for French forces that left Newport, RI on June 9th under the command of General Rochambeau. When the French arrived, the combined armies performed exercises and demonstrations to intimidate the British in New York City. However, Washington and Rochambeau decided that a larger force would be necessary to lay siege to the city. Instead, Washington abandoned his efforts in New York and took half of his forces and the French forces to surround and overwhelm Cornwallis in the south. Clinton in New York would not figure out what Washington was up to for over two weeks and would not send a force out to rescue Cornwallis for another month. Clinton was informed of the surrender enroute and turned back to New York City.

Today, there's a beautiful park on the Hudson at Peekskill. From the park, to the north, you can see where the Hudson squeezes through the Highlands. On the west side of the Hudson was Fort Clinton and Fort Montgomery. On the east side was Fort Independence.

PEEKSKILL TO GARRISON

Mile Mark 4.5 — Reverse direction on Hudson Avenue and depart Peekskill. After going under the US Route 9 bridge, turn right and return back to US Route 9 heading north.

Mile Mark 5.3 — Reach the intersection with US Route 6.

Mile Mark 5.8 — Get over to the left lane and take a left at the light staying on US Route 9 heading north.

Mile Mark 6.1 — Get into the left lane as you approach a rotary. Be sure to yield to traffic in the rotary — they have the right of way. Watch for the Jan Peeck Bridge marker on the right.

Detour onto US Route 6 west, which is about halfway around the rotary. If you miss the exit, go around again. Also, be sure to yield to the Canadian Geese crossing the road.

Mile Mark 6.5 — Pass Camp Smith, a New York National Guard training camp established in 1882.

Jan Peeck Bridge

Named to commemorate the place where Jan Peeck, Dutch trader, 1640-1650 met Indians to trade for furs.

State Education Department 1951

(Peekskill Marker)

Mile Mark 8.8 — As you climb the escarpment on the east side of the Hudson River, watch for the parking lot on the left that affords a scenic view of the Hudson looking south. Carefully, pull into the parking lot and enjoy the view.

Looking north, up the Hudson, one can see the Bear Mountain Bridge. The location of Fort Clinton was just south of the bridge on the western shore. Fort Montgomery was just north of the bridge, also on the western shore.

In October 1777, the British, with a force of about 3,000, moved north against the combined forces of about 600 Americans led by General George Clinton at Forts Clinton and Montgomery. The Americans held the forts until nightfall but after losing almost half of their defenders, they withdrew.

Today, the remains of Fort Montgomery have been cleared and may be seen by visitors.

The Naval Battle of Fort Montgomery

When Sir Henry Clinton's British troops reached Forts Clinton and Montgomery on October 6, 1777, some of his ships began moving upriver to support them. First came two galleys, the *Dependence* and the *Crime*, which were rowed into position. Four American ships, the frigate *Montgomery*, the sloop *Camden*, and the galleys *Shark* and *Lady Washington* defended the giant iron chain the Americans had stretched across the river below Fort Montgomery. As the British galleys approached, a fierce cannon battle ensued. The *Dependence* fired 95 shots from its 24-pounders and many more from its smaller 6-pounders, striking Fort Clinton and the American ships. The American commander held his fire until his ship, the *Montgomery*, was struck. He then returned the fire and ordered the massive 32-pounder cannon on board the *Lady Washington* to do the same. The guns from both forts fired on the British galleys too.

(Continued on page 33)

(Continued from page 32)

Just before the battle reached its climax, two larger British ships, the brig *Diligent* and the sloop tender *Hotham*, and another galley, the *Spitfire*, came into view. Sir Henry Clinton later wrote that the sight of these ships "crowding all sail to support" the attack convinced him to begin his final assault. At dusk, the British drove the Americans from the forts, and the American vessels turned to support their fleeing soldiers. The *Montgomery* saved many Americans from capture by using its cannons to keep the British from encircling the fort. The *Shark*, the *Camden*, and the *Lady Washington* were ordered to rescue as many Americans as possible. As night fell, the ships tried to escape upriver, but the winds were not strong enough to overcome the ebb tide carrying them downriver. The *Camden* was run aground by its crew and was captured by the British. The *Montgomery* and the *Shark* were burned by their crews before they could fall into enemy hands. Only the *Lady Washington* escaped upriver.

(Fort Montgomery Marker)

Carefully pull out of the parking lot and continue west on US Route 6.

The First Chain

Planned to keep British ships from going up river, anchored on shore below, was forced by the enemy, Oct 7, 1777.

State Education
Department 1932

(Route 9D Marker)

Mile Mark 9.6 — Reach the intersection with Route 9D. Bear right at the intersection and detour onto Route 9D heading north.

Mile Mark 10.9 — Watch for the marker on the left for the first chain placed across the Hudson to keep the British from advancing north up the river. Fort Montgomery protected the chain on the west side of the Hudson. Although this chain did not stop the British, a

Sugar Loaf

On the north slope of this hill was one of the forts built, 1776-1777 to defend the Highlands, from Connecticut to New Jersey.

State Education
Department

(US Route 9D Marker)

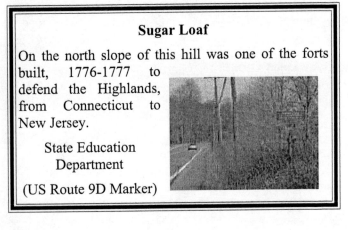

second chain placed at West Point presented a more formidable obstacle.

Mile Mark 12.8 — On the right is a marker for Sugar Loaf, one of many defensive positions placed in the Highlands to keep the British from advancing out of New York City. The fortifications extended from Connecticut to New Jersey.

Mile Mark 13.3 — Watch for Robinson House marker on the right. Just past this marker is the Arnold's flight marker on the left. It was near this point on the Hudson that Benedict Arnold rowed out to the British ship, the "Vulture," to officially become an American traitor.

Mandeville's

This house, built in 1737 was headquarters of commanders of American troops defending West Point, from 1778 to 1783.

State Education
Department

(Garrison Marker)

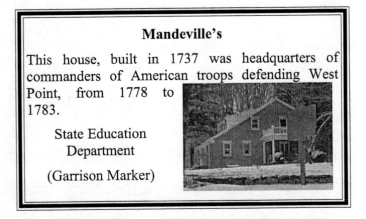

Mile Mark 14.1 — Reach an intersection with Route 403. Turn left and watch for the Mandeville marker on the right.

Mile Mark 14.8 — Reach the stop sign at Upper Station Road. Continue through the intersection and cross the bridge over the railroad tracks. Continue down the west side of the track and find a parking place opposite the train station.

Mile Mark 15.0 — Arrive in the town of Garrison.

GARRISON

The town of Garrison is severed by Amtrak. Noisy, high-speed trains occasionally zoom through the middle of what is normally a very quiet little town. If you're anywhere near the tracks when one comes through, it will scare you half-to-death.

Private property restricts access to the Hudson River, but look for a pagoda where the public is invited. From the pagoda, the United States Military Academy at West Point can be seen clearly across the river.

The Great Chain

The Hudson River's narrow width and sharp turns at West Point created adverse sailing conditions and prompted construction of a great chain in 1778 as an obstacle to the movement of British ships north of this point. American soldiers positioned the chain to impede the progress of a ship should it attempt to turn into the east-west channel against frequently unfavorable winds and a strong current. Cannon were placed in forts and batteries on both sides of the river to destroy the ship as it slowed to a halt against the obstacle.

When finally completed, the 600-yard chain contained iron links two feet in length and weighing 114 pounds, including swivels, clevises, and

(Continued on page 38)

(Continued from page 37)

anchors, the chain weighed 65 tons. For buoyancy, 40-foot logs were cut into 16-foot sections, waterproofed, and joined by fours into rafts fastened with 12-foot timbers. Short sections of chain (ten links and a clevis) were stapled across each raft. Later the chain sections were united.

On 30 April 1778, Captain Thomas Machin, the engineer responsible for assembling and installing the obstruction, eased the chain across the river, anchoring its northern end under the protection of Marine Battery on Constitution Island. The southern end was secured in a small cove guarded by Chain Battery at the river's edge. Both ends were anchored to log cribs filled with rocks. A system of pulleys, rollers, ropes, and mid-stream anchors adjusted the chain's tension to overcome the effects of river current and changing tide. Until 1783, the chain was removed each winter and reinstalled each spring to avoid destruction by ice. A log "boom" (resembling a ladder in construction) also spanned the river about 100 yards downstream to absorb the initial impact of a ship attempting to penetrate the barrier. Several links of the chain are located at trophy point. A section of the boom was recovered from the river in 1855 and is on display at Washington's headquarters museum in Newburgh.

The British fleet never approached West Point, and the strength of the great chain was never tested.

(West Point Marker)

At this "west point" on the Hudson, Fort Arnold, later renamed Fort Clinton, once stood. Its strategic position can be clearly seen from Garrison. The fort overlooked the entire bend that the river makes at this point.

In 1778, a second, "great chain" was stretched across the Hudson at West Point. Links from the actual chain can be seen at West Point. There is also a marker at the point that tells about the chain.

GARRISON TO COLD SPRING

Mile Mark 15.0 — Depart Garrison and recross the bridge over the railroad tracks. Bear left onto Upper Station Road to get back to Route 9D.

Mile Mark 15.6 — Reach the intersection with Route 9D. The intersection is not marked. Turn left going north.

Mile Mark 16.1 — Watch for the Connecticut camps marker on the right. The camps were a part of the defense set up in the Highlands during the Revolution.

Mile Mark 17.7 — Reach the Connecticut Line marker on the right.

Mile Mark 18.1 — Pass Boscobel on the left. Boscobel is a fully restored, early 19th century home overlooking the Hudson.

Mile Mark 18.7 — Watch for the speed limit change as you enter the village of Cold Spring. Detour briefly onto Peekskill Road on the right just after the speed limit change.

Mile Mark 19.0 — Turn right onto Main Street in Nelsonville.

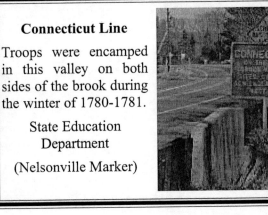

Connecticut Line

Troops were encamped in this valley on both sides of the brook during the winter of 1780-1781.

State Education Department

(Nelsonville Marker)

1/2 Mile — Army Camp

While West Point defences were being built in 1781, the Connecticut Line encamped along the brook.

New York State Education Department 1932

(Route 9D Marker)

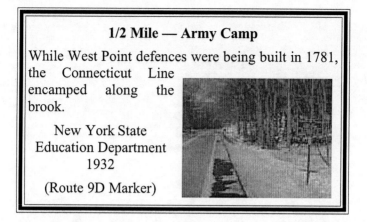

Mile Mark 19.3 — Watch for the Connecticut Line marker on the right. This area was also part of the defense set up in the Highlands.

Reverse direction on Main Street and proceed west through the village of Nelsonville to Cold Spring.

Mile Mark 20.5 — Reach the intersection with Route 9D. Proceed straight through the intersection.

Mile Mark 20.8 — Reach the railroad tracks that, like Garrison, splits Cold Spring. Turn left and take the bridge over the tracks. Arrive in Cold Spring.

Connecticut Camps

On the hill west of the brook are remains of hut sites, ovens, etc., made by New England troops guarding West Point, 1778-1781.

State Education Department

(Route 9D Marker)

COLD SPRING

If you turn left onto Market Street, you can return back to Main Street and go to a small park on the Hudson River near the Hudson House River Inn. From the park, you get a nice view of Constitution Island.

If you turn right onto Market Street and proceed into the commuter parking lot near the train station, there is a small park that affords a closer view of Constitution Island. There is a Warner Sisters marker in the park. A visit to both sites is recommended.

Constitution Island, which is just north of West Point, played an important role in the defense of the Hudson

Warner Sisters

View to Constitution Island preserved by authors Susan Warner & Anna Warner who wrote the hymn "Jesus Loves Me." C. 1818-1915.

George E. Pataki, Governor

(Cold Spring Marker)

River and the Highlands on either side. Today, railroad tracks cut access to the island, making it only accessible by water.

Constitution Island

In 1775, the first American patriots occupied Martelaer's Rock and soon renamed it Constitution Island after the British Constitution. In 1775, the Americans built Roman's battery on the island. This was the first fortification in the West Point area. By the end of 1776, they also built Marine Battery, Hillcliff Battery and Gravel Hill Battery. In 1777, the British destroyed these positions.

In 1778 and 1779, the Americans partially rebuilt Marine Battery, completely rebuilt Gravel Hill Battery, and constructed three interior redoubts to protect the river batteries from attack from the north. These fortifications added depth to the West Point defensive zone.

In 1778, the great chain was anchored at Constitution Island in the cove below Marine Battery.

(West Point Marker)

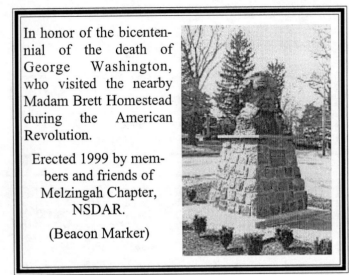

In honor of the bicentennial of the death of George Washington, who visited the nearby Madam Brett Homestead during the American Revolution.

Erected 1999 by members and friends of Melzingah Chapter, NSDAR.

(Beacon Marker)

COLD SPRING TO FISHKILL

Mile Mark 21.8 — Return to Main Street and turn left onto Fair Street. Proceed up Fair Street to Route 9D.

Mile Mark 22.5 — Reach the intersection with Route 9D. Turn left going north to Fishkill.

Mile Mark 23.8 — Pass through a tunnel under the Highlands and proceed up the east side of the Hudson aware of the scenic view on the western shore.

Mile Mark 28.4 — Enter the city of Beacon. Watch for the George Washington statue on the left. In August 1775, General Washington visited this area to study the defense of the Hudson. Later, across the river in Newburgh, he headquartered at the Hasbrouck house while America awaited the Paris peace treaty in 1783. The house still stands today and is open for visitors.

Mile Mark 30.3 — Cross over Interstate 84.

Mile Mark 30.6 — Watch for the Mount Gulian marker on the left. Get into the left lane and turn left.

FISHKILL

During the Revolution, Fishkill was the site of a large supply depot. The depot supplied the northern department of the Continental Army, who were responsible for securing the Highlands and keeping the British from moving north of New York City. There are several historical sites to see in the Fishkill area. The first is here at Mount Gulian.

Mount Gulian — The homestead is reached by entering Hudson View Park and making an immediate left on Lamplight Street. Mount Gulian is past an apartment complex at the end of the road about a half-mile from Route 9D.

Verplanck House

Built 1740, by Gulian Verplanck. Burned 1931. Headquarters Baron Steuben, 1782. Society of Cincinnati organized here in 1783.

State Education Department

(Fishkill Marker)

Mount Gulian

Built about 1750 by Gulian Ver Planck whose ancestors and Francis Rombout purchased the adjacent land from the Wappinger Indians in 1605.

Headquarters of Baron Von Steuben. The Society for the Cincinnati was instituted here May 1765.

Placed by the Colonial Dames of the State of New York. MDCCCXCIX

(Mount Gulian Marker)

The Mount Gulian, Ver Planck homestead is a circa 1740 Dutch colonial overlooking the Hudson. During the final days of the Revolution, it was the headquarters of General von Steuben, inspector general of the Continental Army in 1783. Steuben is given credit for turning the Continental Army into a strong, fighting force with his training at Valley Forge.

In 1783, the nation's first veterans group, the Society of the Cincinnati, was formed at the Mount Gulian site.

Washington's Sword

Now in the Smithsonian Institution, Washington, DC, was made near here by John Bailey, a cutler from New York and Fishkill.

State Education Department

(Fishkill Marker)

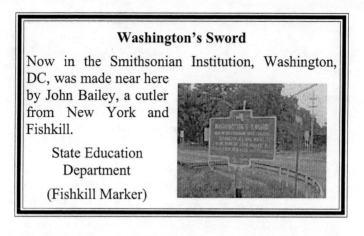

Today, the Mount Gulian homestead offers educational programs and special events for the public to enjoy. For example, in September, they offer a Revolutionary War living history weekend with special visits by George Washington and Thomas Jefferson.

Washington's Sword — The sword marker can be reached by returning to Route 9D north for about a mile and a half, turning right onto Route 36 for another mile and a half and turning left onto Route 52 for about two miles. On Route 36, you will pass by New York State correctional facilities. The Washington Sword marker is in the northwest corner of the intersection with Interstate 84.

Dutch Reformed Church — The church can be reached by following Route 52 through the center of Fishkill. As you approach US Route 9, the Dutch Reformed Church is on the left. The church housed prisoners of war during the American Revolution. Between September 1776 and February 1777, it served as the seat of state government when the British forced the New York Provincial Congress out of New York City and White Plains.

Dutch Church

Reformed church of Fishkill, organized 1716, built 1725 occupied 1776 by New York Provincial Congress, also a prison during Revolution.

State Education Department 1935

(Church Marker)

✝

Trinity Church

Organized in communion with the Church of England by the Rev. Samuel Seabury, 1756. The first rector Rev. John Beardsley, Oct. 26, 1766. Reincorporated, Oct. 13, 1785 and Oct. 16, 1796. This building was erected about 1769. Occupied by the New York Provincial Convention which was removed from White Plains, Sept. 3, 1776. Used for a military hospital by the army of General Washington until disbanded, June 2, 1783. Pro Deo et Patria, 1756 — 1894.

(Church Marker)

First Reformed Dutch Church of Fishkill

Organized 1710. Building erected 1731. Provincial Convention met here 1776. Used as a military prison during the Revolution. Enlarged 1786. Interior remodeled 1806, 1820, 1854, 1882.

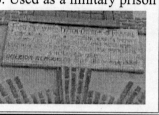

(Church Marker)

Trinity Episcopal Church — Just across the intersection with Route 9 on the right is the Trinity

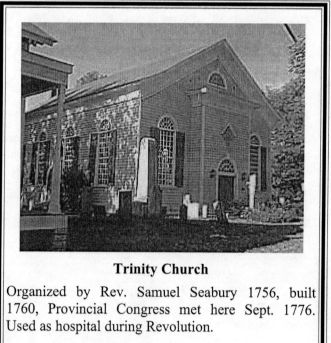

Trinity Church

Organized by Rev. Samuel Seabury 1756, built 1760, Provincial Congress met here Sept. 1776. Used as hospital during Revolution.

Sate Education Department

(Church Marker)

Episcopal Church. The church also served as a temporary home for the New York State government and as a military hospital.

Van Wyck Homestead — The homestead can be reached by following US Route 9 south for about a mile and making a left at the light just after the intersection with Interstate 84. The Van Wyck

Homestead is tucked between this intersection and the interstate.

The homestead is a restored Dutch colonial that housed officers of Washington's army. It was also the army's northern supply depot headquarters and is reputedly the setting for James Fennimore Cooper's The Spy. It contains portraits by Ammi Phillips as well as artifacts from the Fishkill Depot and Barracks.

1776 * 1976

**American Revolution
Bicentennial Memorial**

To all the braves souls who passed through, served, and died here at the site of the Northern Department Supply Depot, Fishkill, New York, 1776-1783.

May their spirit of dedication be rekindled within the souls of all who stop, reflect, and journey on. Dedicated July 4, 1954

(Van Wyck Marker)

1776-1783

In grateful remembrance of the brave men who gave their lives for their country during the American Revolution and whose remains repose in the adjoining field.

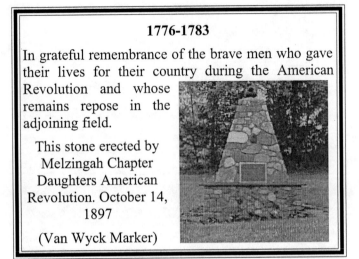

This stone erected by
Melzingah Chapter
Daughters American
Revolution. October 14,
1897

(Van Wyck Marker)

Today, the Van Wyck Homestead is obviously near the intersection of two very busy highways, US Route 9

Great Indian Warrior

Trading Path

The most heavily traveled road in Colonial America passed through here, linking areas from the Great Lakes to Augusta, GA. Laid on ancient animal and Native American Trading/Warrior Paths, Indian treaties among the governors of NY, PA, and VA and the 19 chiefs of Iroquois League of Five Nations in 1685 and 1722, opened the colonial backcountry for peaceful settlement and colonization. In NY, the path linked the Iroquois and the Great Lakes to the major eastern trails and tribes for trade, hunting and war.

National Society Daughters of the American Colonists. Project of the 2000-3 Administration.

(Van Wyck Marker)

and I84. In colonial times the homestead was on the old Post Road. A Post Road marker can be seen just south of the house near the shopping center. A marker at the homestead describes the Indian trading path that existed here prior to colonial times.

Mile Mark 38.3 — Depart the Van Wyck Homestead and head north on US Route 9.

Mile Mark 43.7 — Watch for the sign to the village of Wappingers Falls on the left. It's past the McDonalds

Mesier Park

Pre-Revolutionary home of the Mesier family from 1777 to 1890 acquired by village 1891.

On May 1, 1777, this dwelling with a farm of about four hundred and twenty two acres of land on which it stood was conveyed to Peter Mesier of New York City by Nicholas Brewer, who had owned the property since October 9, 1741. It became the residence of the Mesier family and was known as the Mesier homestead until August 27, 1891, when it was conveyed with a plot of five acres of the land to the village of Wappingers Falls under an agreement that the property should be forever known as Mesier Park.

State Education Department 1935

(Wappingers Falls Markers)

and just before the Dairy Queen. This old country road is a relief from the stop and go traffic on US Route 9.

Mile Mark 44.1 — Reach the town of Wappingers Falls. Pass Mesier Park on the right and take the right into the park. Loop around the park so you can get a close look at the 18th century, Mesier Homestead inside the park.

Return back to the light in front of the homestead and proceed straight onto Route 9D heading north through the village and over the falls.

Mile Mark 45.7 — Reach the intersection with US Route 9. Turn left heading north.

Mile Mark 48.9 — IBM Corporation is on the left side of US Route 9. At one time, IBM and Poughkeepsie were synonymous — not anymore. Poughkeepsie is still reeling from IBM's workforce reductions.

Mile Mark 49.7 — Pass Locust Grove, the former home of Samuel F. B. Morse on the left — the inventor of the Morse Code.

Mile Mark 50.4 — Reach the exit for Academy Street. Turn right heading into the city of Poughkeepsie.

Mile Mark 51.6 — Reach downtown Poughkeepsie. Turn right onto Church Street, which is US Route 44 east.

Mile Mark 52.5 — Get into the left lane and exit US Route 44 by turning left onto Worrall Avenue (Route 115). Go about a block and turn left on Main Street.

Mile Mark 52.8 — Watch for the Glebe House on the right just across the intersection with Church Street.

POUGHKEEPSIE

Glebe House — The Glebe House, circa 1767, was built as a parsonage for the Anglican Church. It was home to Rev. John Beardsley of Trinity Church in Fishkill and Christ Church in Poughkeepsie. Beardsley was exiled to Canada during the Revolution for his loyalist sympathies. After the exile, the home was used by Continental Army officers.

Clinton House — The Clinton House, circa 1765, is about a quarter mile west of the Glebe House at the northwest corner of North White Street and Main Street. During the Revolution, the house was often used by New York Governor George Clinton during visits to the Poughkeepsie area. Today, the Clinton

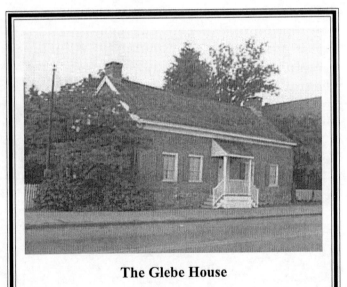

The Glebe House

Built in 1767 by members of the Church of England in Dutchess County for their ministers.

State Education Department 1935

(Poughkeepsie Marker)

House is administered by the Dutchess County Historical Society. In the house, exhibits present the history of Dutchess County.

The Frigates *Montgomery* and the *Congress* — Two frigates that participated in the naval battle at Fort Montgomery were constructed on the Hudson River in Poughkeepsie. The river area where the ships were constructed can be reached by following US Route 44 west until you reach the intersection with US Route 9. US Route 44 West is a block north of the Clinton House.

On December 13, 1775, Congress authorized the construction of the frigates Completed in November of 1776, the *Congress* weighed 682 tons and was rated at 28 guns with a deck length of 126 feet. The *Montgomery* weighed 563 tons and was rated at 24 guns with a deck length of 119 feet. In July of 1777, the two ships were sent down the Hudson to bolster the defenses at the first chain, which crossed the Hudson near Fort Montgomery. Although rated higher, the *Montgomery* carried only 8 12-pounder cannons and the *Congress* carried 9 9-pounder cannons. The ships were unable to stop the British attack on Fort Montgomery because the British chose to attack overland. After the British took Fort Montgomery, the two ships did not escape and both were set on fire to prevent them from falling into enemy hands, thus concluding a very short history for both ships. However, they both helped to keep Clinton cautious about a major invasion up the Hudson from New York City.

POUGHKEEPSIE TO RHINEBECK

Mile Mark 54.3 — Depart Poughkeepsie on US Route 9 heading north.

Mile Mark 55.8 — Pass Marist College on the left. Began as a religious training school for the order of the Marist Brothers; today it is a popular college of the arts and sciences.

Mile Mark 57.7 — Pass the CIA (the Culinary Institute of America) on the left — where America's best chefs learn their trade. The CIA has several restaurants; reservations are a must.

Mile Mark 58.4 — Keep to the left. The lane on the right leads onto Route 9G, which goes to Eleanor Roosevelt's home, Valkill.

Mile Mark 59.3 — Pass the home of Franklin Delano Roosevelt on the left.

Mile Mark 61.2 — Pass the Vanderbilt Mansion, also on the left.

Mile Mark 62.9 — Pass a Post Road marker on the left.

Mile Mark 70.5 — Arrive in Rhinebeck.

Landsman's Kill

Whose waters operated the mills of Schuyler, Montgomery, Morgan, Lewis, Livingston and many others.

New York State
Education Department
1932

(Rhinebeck Marker)

RHINEBECK

During the Revolution, Rhinebeck, a part of the "Breadbasket of Dutchess County," provided badly needed flour and grain to the American troops who were stationed in the Highlands to

Rhinebeck Reformed Church

Serving Christ and our community since 1731.

(Rhinebeck Church Marker)

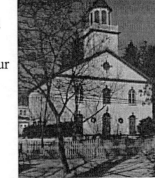

Revolutionary soldiers buried here.

Placed here by the NY State Organization NSDAR.

(Rhinebeck Marker)

the south. In all, Dutchess County provided about one-third of all the grain consumed by the Americans.

In June 1775, Henry Beekman Livingston formed a company of local militia. The company drilled on the lawn of the Bogardus Tavern, today's Beekman Arms, the oldest, still active tavern in America. In August, General George

Bogardus Land

Training ground of Revolutionary Forces. Formerly belonged to William Traphagen, founder of village of Rhinebeck.

State Education Department 1932

(Rhinebeck Marker)

Beekman Arms

Landlords of
"America's Oldest Inn"

William Traphagen — 1766-1769
Everadus Bogardus — 1769-1802
Asa Potter — 1802-1805
William Jacques — 1805-1835
Mrs. Jaqucs — 1835-1837
Jacob H. Tremper — 1837-1840
Robert T. Seymour — 1840-1852
O.V. Doty — 1853-1855
Frederick Sipperly — 1855-1857
Edward Pultz — 1857-1858
Hunting Germond — 1858-1860
Burnett Conkling — 1860-1862
Jas. N. McElroy — 1862-1864
Griffin Hoffman — 1864-1873
Tremper Brothers — 1873-1884
Lorenzo Decker — 1884-1891
Edward Lasher — 1891-1893
E.M. Vanderburgh — 1893-1894
Vernon D. Lake — 1894-1906
Halleek Welles — 1906-1907
Arthur Shuffle — 1907-1914
Wallace W. Foster — 1914-1926
Beckman Arms, Inc. — 1926-1930
Lewis F. Winne — 1930-1950
Kenneth Arnold — 1950-1952
Howard Hohl — 1952-1953
Walter Harter — 1954-1958
Charles LaForge, Jr. — 1958-

(Beekman Arms Marker)

Washington came to inspect the company and the area's defenses. Washington had just been appointed commander of the Continental Army and he suspected that the British would try to control the Hudson Valley. Legend has it that he stayed at the Bogardus Tavern.

This stone marks the crossing of the Kings Highway and the Sepasco Indian Trail, later named the Ulster and Salisbury Turnpike, over which traveled the Connecticut Pioneers to their new homes in western New York.

Erected by Chancellor Livingston Chapter Daughters of the American Revolution 1922

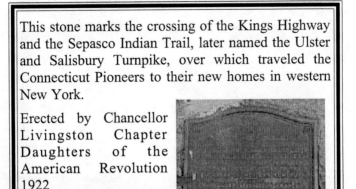

(Rhinebeck Marker)

RHINEBECK TO REDHOOK

Mile Mark 70.5 — Depart Rhinebeck heading north on US Route 9. Note the Kings Highway marker at the northwest corner of the intersection at Rhinebeck's center.

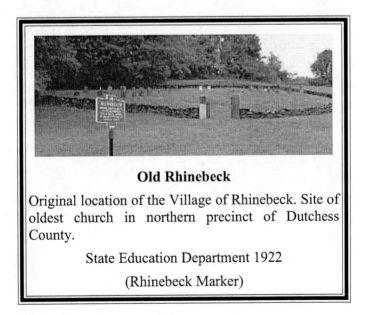

Old Rhinebeck

Original location of the Village of Rhinebeck. Site of oldest church in northern precinct of Dutchess County.

State Education Department 1922

(Rhinebeck Marker)

The Evangelical Lutheran Church of St. Peter the Apostle known for more than a century as the Stone Church within its walls stood the first church built in 1730 by the Palatine settlers to whose memory this tablet is erected by Chancellor Livingston Chapter Daughters of the American Revolution and the state of New York 1925.

(Church Marker)

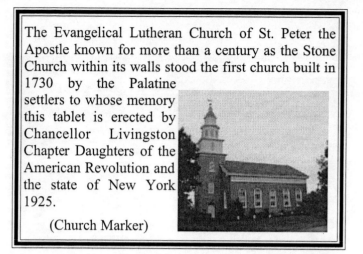

Mile Mark 72.7 — Reach the intersection with Route 9G. Watch for a cemetery on the right with a marker that identifies the original location of the village of Rhinebeck.

Mile Mark 73.4 — The Evangelical Lutheran Church of St. Peter the Apostle is on the left. There is a marker on the church.

Mile Mark 75.7 — Reach the intersection with Route 199 and the center of Red Hook.

Just past the intersection with Route 199 on the right is the Silk City Diner. There is a marker in front of the diner identifying it as the first diner in New York State and the fourth in the country. It has the classic coach style with a counter and booths.

Elmendorph Inn — Just past the diner is the Elmendorph Inn. The inn was a stagecoach stop on the Albany-New York Post Road. No doubt, the inn and the diner provide evidence that Red Hook has been extending its hospitality to visitors for over 200 years.

Van Ness House — The house can be reached by returning back to Route 199 and heading west about a half-mile.

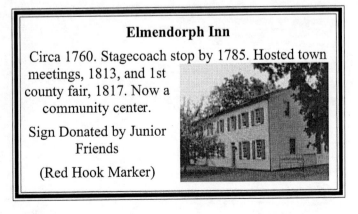

Elmendorph Inn

Circa 1760. Stagecoach stop by 1785. Hosted town meetings, 1813, and 1st county fair, 1817. Now a community center.

Sign Donated by Junior Friends

(Red Hook Marker)

> ### David Van Ness
>
> Built brick house here before 1797, was captain during Revolution, General of State Militia, State Senator and Presidential Elector, 1812.
>
> State Education
> Department
>
> (Red Hook Marker)

During the Revolution, many patriots from Red Hook stepped forward to participate in the Continental Army and the local militia. David Van Ness was a Revolutionary War Officer and a marker stands at the location of his home.

Another prominent figure during the Revolution was Egbert Benson. Benson had attended Kings College with fellow classmates Robert Livingston, John Jay and Alexander Hamilton. In Red Hook, Benson was the leader of the local militia and was responsible for recruiting soldiers for the Continental Army.

RED HOOK TO CLERMONT

Mile Mark 76.6 — Depart Red Hook heading west on Route 199.

Mile Mark 78.0 — Reach the intersection with Route 9G. Turn right on Route 9G heading north.

Mile Mark 78.9 — Pass the road to Montgomery Place on the left.

The original house at Montgomery Place was destroyed by the British after the burning of Kingston during the 1777 invasion from New York City. Janet Livingston Montgomery, widow of General Richard Montgomery, built the current home in 1804.

General Montgomery was one of the first generals commissioned in the Continental Army. He served under Philip Schuyler, the commander of the Northern Department of the Continental Army, in a 1775 expedition against British-held Quebec. When Schuyler became ill, Montgomery took command of the expedition and was killed leading a winter assault against the well-defended fortress of Quebec.

Janet Livingston Montgomery was the sister of Chancellor Robert Livingston of Clermont. The Livingston Homestead, "Clermont," is the next stop on our Revolutionary War road trip.

Historic Hudson Valley

Montgomery Place

(Montgomery Place Entrance)

Mile Mark 79.4 — Pass Bard College on the left. Bard College was founded by the Episcopal Church in 1860. Today, it is an elite college for the study of the arts and sciences with emphasis on the arts.

Mile Mark 82.7 — Watch for the Red Church on the left. The church, established in 1766, was a witness to the British invasion but was spared. It is likely, however, that if the British knew the church's ties to the  Livingston family, the church would have been burned to the ground.

Mile Mark 83.7 — Watch for the directional sign to Clermont. Turn left, as directed, to Clermont.

A few miles further north on Route 9G is Germantown. The town has many historical sites including a parsonage that dates back to the 1740's. A visit to Germantown is recommended on a longer visit to the area.

Mile Mark 84.5 — Watch for the Clermont marker up on right. Continue past the marker toward the visitor center.

Mile Mark 85.5 — Arrive at Clermont.

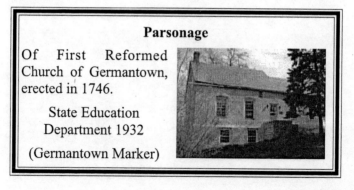

Parsonage

Of First Reformed Church of Germantown, erected in 1746.

State Education
Department 1932

(Germantown Marker)

CLERMONT

Although Clermont is quiet today, in the 18th century, it was a center of political and social activity led by the prominent Livingston family.

Livingston Manor — The Clermont estate was established here in 1728 and remained in the family for seven successive generations — 230 years.

In October 1777, Major John Vaughan came to Clermont and burned Livingston's home because of his prominent role in support of independence. Margaret

Clermont

Built 1730, on Livingston Manor. Home of Chancellor Livingston, one of the five drafters of the Declaration of Independence.

(Clermont Marker)

> ## Robert R. Livingston
> ### Born 1746 — Died 1813
>
> Recorder of New York, 1773-1775, Member of Continental Congress, 1775-77, 1779-81, 1784-85, On committee of five which drafted Declaration of Independence, Member of Provincial Congress, 1775-77, Chancellor of New York, 1777-1801, Secretary of Foreign Affairs, 1781-1783, Minister to France, 1801-04, Negotiator of Louisiana Purchase, Administered Oath to George Washington as first President of United States, 1789, Shared with Robert Fulton invention of steamboat and its navigation, Grand Master of Grand Lodge of Free and Accepted Masons of New York State, 1784-1801.
>
> Erected by Masonic Lodges of 2nd Columbia-Dutchess District and State of New York
>
> (Clermont Marker)

Beekman Livingston rebuilt the family home between 1779 and 1782. This was the furthest north that Clinton's 1777 invasion from New York City reached.

Robert R. Livingston, son of Judge Robert R. Livingston and Margaret Beekman served with Thomas Jefferson as a member of the committee that drafted the Declaration of Independence. He took office as Secretary of Foreign Affairs in 1781 after it took Congress over nine months to select a candidate for the position.

Chancellor Livingston concluded his public career as Thomas Jefferson's Minister to France between 1801 and 1804. While in Paris, he negotiated the Louisiana Purchase and entered into a partnership with Robert Fulton, a Pennsylvania-born painter and inventor who shared Livingston's fascination with steam navigation.

71

The road, paralleling Clermont's main parking lot, was laid out in the 18th century by Chancellor Robert R. Livingston. The road received its name from the beautiful locust trees that grew on either side.

(Clermont Marker)

Their creation, which they called the *North River*, is known to history as the *Clermont*. Their steamboat embarked on its maiden voyage between New York City and Albany in 1807,  setting off a transportation revolution in the United States.

Today, the visitor center and mansion are open between mid April and Labor Day — Wednesday thru

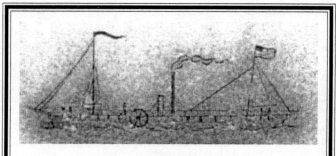

Clermont

Since and prior to its incorporation in 1788, Clermont has played a significant role in the history of America. Clermont's history includes the home of Robert R. Livingston, negotiator of the Louisiana Purchase and a drafter of the Declaration of Independence. Birthplace of Philip Livingston, a signer of the Declaration of Independence. Home of Edward Livingston, Secretary of State under Jackson. Site of the first public school and one of the first 100 post offices in 1791. Home of the academy in 1834 and the first agricultural fair in 1819. Home of the first steamboat, the Clermont, built by Robert Fulton in 1807 and backed by R.R. Livingston with pride in Clermont's History and hope and expectation. For the future, we the Livingston Manor Grange, established 1905, dedicate this monument, July 17, 1976.

(Clermont Marker)

Saturdays from 10AM until 5PM and Sundays Noon until 5PM. From Labor Day until the end of October — Wednesdays thru Sundays Noon until 5PM. The visitor center and mansion are also open on Monday holidays during the season from 10AM until 5PM.

Clermont Village — The village of Clermont is on US Route 9. You can reach the village, which is about six

miles to the east, by returning back to the intersection with Route 9G and following the winding Route 6 across the intersection, past Cedar Run and Werner Farms to the intersection with Route 9.

Just north of this intersection on the left is a marker indicating that Clermont had one of the first post offices in the United States. Further north on the left is a marker that indicates that Clermont had one of the first public schools. Although Clermont is tiny, a marker at the old academy notes that it is very big in history.

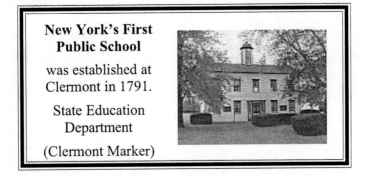

Old Red Brick Tavern known in 1789 as the **T h o m a s   H o u s e** ; headquarters in 1777 of General Putnam

State Education Department 1932

(Upper Red Hook Marker)

Upper Red Hook — In October of 1777, General Putnam made Upper Red Hook (just south of Clermont off US Route 9) his temporary headquarters while he shadowed the British invasion up the Hudson from New York City.

When Putnam received word that Burgoyne had surrendered to Gates at Saratoga, ending the British invasion from Canada, he sent a dispatch from Red Hook to General Washington informing him of the victory. Gates, who had desires to replace Washington as Commander-in-Chief, delivered his victory dispatch not to Washington, but directly to the Continental Congress.

Blue Store

W. T. Livingston and L. Ten Broeck, early proprietors. Name derived from store and tavern painted blue.

(Blue Store Marker)

CLERMONT TO LIVINGSTON

Mile Mark 91.9 — Depart Clermont and proceed north on US Route 9.

Mile Mark 93.5 — Watch for the Blue Stores Hotel and Restaurant on the left.

Today, the building is red and white, but blue lettering can be found on the sign. Inside, antiques are a part of the restaurant décor and can

Highland Turnpike

Incorporated in 1804. An early road.

State Education Department

(Blue Store Marker)

be seen standing, mounted and hanging everywhere.

On weekends, the restaurant is a recommended stop for lunch or on a longer visit to the area, it's a recommended stop for dinner.

The town of Blue Store is a colonial crossroad. It is at the intersection of the old Albany-New York Post Road and the Highland Turnpike.

Mile Mark 96.4 — Reach the town of Livingston.

Welcome to the town of

Livingston

organized 1788, Robert Livingston, 1st Lord of the Manor of Livingston.

(Livingston Marker)

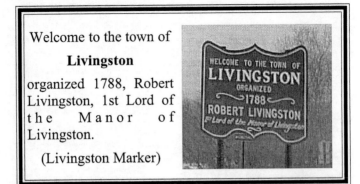

LIVINGSTON

At the entrance to Livingston, there is a post road marker and a town marker. The post road marker indicates 116 miles to New York.

The town center can be reached by bearing right at the post road marker and

1656 - 1727

Alida Livingston, a capable courageous and diligent manager of her husband's manor, she helped to settle Columbia County.

George E. Pataki, Governor

(Livingston Marker)

Livingston

The present village of Livingston was formerly called Johnstown after John Livingston.

State Education Department 1935

(Livingston Marker)

taking a brief detour through this scenic and historic town. There are several historic markers in the center of the town, a town created by Robert Livingston.

Johnstown

Named for John Livingston, settler. Livingston post office 1805. Had a revolutionary stage inn and Linlithgo Reformed Church.

State Education Department 1935

(Livingston Marker)

LIVINGSTON TO CLAVERACK

Mile Mark 97.3 — Depart Livingston and return back to US Route 9 heading north.

Mile Mark 98.1 — Pass the stone house farm on the left and a post road marker.

Mile Mark 99.3 — Reach the intersection with Route 9H. Continue straight through the intersection and make a detour on Route 9H heading north.

Mile Mark 102.8 — Watch for Claverack Creek. Take the first right after the creek onto Shaw Bridge Road.

Mile Mark 103.0 — Watch for a classic, Dutch style home on the left at the intersection of Shaw Bridge Road and Van Wyck Road. Turn left onto Van Wyck and when you reach a four way stop, continue going straight.

Mile Mark 103.6 — Reach the intersection with Route 23. Turn left, heading west.

Mile Mark 103.8 — Watch for the Lower Manor marker on the right.

Mile Mark 104.2 — Reach the intersection with Route 9H. Continue through the intersection, heading west.

The Lower Manor

Location of the lower manor of Van Rensselaer Patroonship. House built by Hendrick Van Rensselaer in 1685. Tenants paid rents here.

(Claverack Marker)

Note the beautiful old homes of Claverack.

Mile Mark 104.6 — Reach the intersection with Old Lane Road. Arrive at the First Court House in Claverack.

First Court House

Erected 1788, Alexander Hamilton, Aaron Burr, other prominent lawyers tried cases here. Martin Van Buren admitted to bar here. Court moved to Hudson in 1805.

Columbia County Grangers 1960.

(Claverack Marker)

CLAVERACK

At the first court house, a marker indicates that Alexander Hamilton and Aaron Burr tried cases here. Before they were trying cases, both were veterans of the American Revolution.

Alexander Hamilton formed an artillery company in 1775. He served under George Washington and in March 1777, at the age of 20, he became George Washington's Aide-de-Camp. After the Revolution, Hamilton helped lead the efforts to create a constitutional convention and served as the first Secretary of the Treasury under President Washington.

Washington Seminary

Early Columbia County school established here 1779. Later became Claverack College and Hudson River Institute until its closing in 1902.

(Claverack Marker)

During the Revolution, Aaron Burr was with Benedict Arnold during an attempted invasion of Canada. He also wintered with Washington at Valley Forge. Later in races for President and Governor of New York, Aaron Burr was defeated, in part due to the efforts of Alexander Hamilton, which led to a growing hatred for each other. This eventually led to the famous gun duel in 1804 in which Hamilton was killed.

Two additional historic sites can be found by returning to Route 9H north. A short distance past the intersection with Route 23 is the Washington Seminary and the Reformed Dutch Church. Both have markers on Route 9H.

Reformed Dutch Church of Claverack

Congregation established, 1716. Current sanctuary built, 1767. NYS historical register, May 5, 2001. National register, June 21, 2001.

(Claverack Marker)

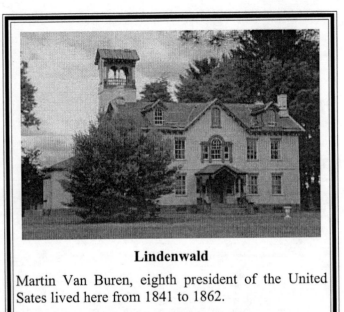

Lindenwald

Martin Van Buren, eighth president of the United Sates lived here from 1841 to 1862.

(Lindenwald Marker)

CLAVERACK TO KINDERHOOK

Mile Mark 105.3 — Depart Claverack heading north on Route 9H.

Mile Mark 108.4 — Reach the intersection with Route 66. East of this intersection is the town of Chatham, a historic town with a Shaker museum and many 19th century buildings and homes.

Mile Mark 115.4 — Watch for the post road marker on the left and the home of Martin Van Buren, eighth president of the United States. Van Buren was born at the end of the Revolution in 1782 in Kinderhook.

There are several markers about Martin Van Buren and his home, Lindenwald. Missing from the markers is the legendary roots of the commonly used response, "OK."

Martin Van Buren

National Park Service, Department of Interior
Lindenwald and the Old Post Road

Van Buren's purchase in 1839 of this property and the 1797 home marked the return of land formerly owned by his ancestors and made the sitting President the owner of a stately home he had admired and visited as a young lawyer.

Van Buren likely had many reasons for choosing the home, which he renamed "Lindenwald" — German for "linden forest." The home came with 137 acres, which later grew to 220. Here he could establish a farm, be near his family and friends and — importantly for prominent politicians — the home was located on the Old Post Road. At the time Martin Van Buren bought this property, the Old Post Road was the main thoroughfare between the state capital of Albany and New York City. Prominent citizens and politicians having business in Albany would stop at Lindenwald to pay their respects to former President Van Buren.

After losing his bid for reelection, Van Buren retired here in 1841. He made many changes to the house while here. In 1849-50 he hired prominent architect Richard Upjohn to design changes. Among the many changes Upjohn designed were additions to the south and west sides of the house, construction of the 63-foot high tower and the addition of the two gatehouses at each end of the drive. You are standing near the south gatehouse.

(Lindenwald Marker)

Martin Van Buren

National Park Service Department of Interior

In 1782, six years after the English colonies in North America declared independence from the British Crown, Martin Van Buren was born to a successful tavern owner and his wife in the village of Kinderhook, NY. At the age of 14 he apprenticed with a local attorney and was admitted to the bar in November 1803.

As a lawyer, Van Buren became familiar with politicians and the issues of the day and was soon involved in Columbia County politics, winning his first election in 1807. He progressed to the state senate from 1812-21, voting to support the War of 1812, working to extend voting rights, rewriting the state constitution and abolishing debtors' prisons. In the U.S. Senate from 1821-1828, he favored a strict interpretation of the Constitution, urging that Congress not finance internal improvements such as roads and canals. Van Buren befriended Andrew Jackson and campaigned for him in 1828. In turn, President Jackson requested Van Buren's assistance as Secretary of State, appointed him Minister to Great Britain and ran with him as his Vice Presidential candidate for the second term.

During the Van Buren Administration (1837-41), the Independent Treasury system brought order to the national economy while his foreign policy avoided war with Mexico. Failing reelection in 1840, Martin Van Buren retired to Lindenwald to be near lifelong friends and establish a large farm. On July 24, 1862, the country's flags flew at half-mast upon the death

(Continued on page 87)

(Continued from page 86)

of Martin Van Buren. In and around Kinderhook the people of Columbia County mourned the loss of "... an old neighbor, a kind friend, and a very esteemed citizen."

(Lindenwald Marker)

Apparently, Van Buren signed off his documents with "OK," referring to "Old Kinderhook."

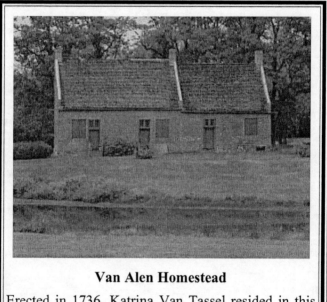

Van Alen Homestead

Erected in 1736, Katrina Van Tassel resided in this house according to tradition.

State Education Department

(Kinderhook Marker)

Post Road—1772

Albany to New York. Weekly mail service established on horseback. Passenger service by covered wagons and four horses in 1786.

State Education
Department

(Kinderhook Marker)

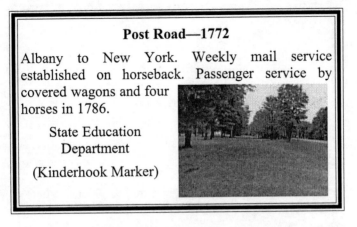

Mile Mark 116.2 — Just past Kinderhook Toyota is the Van Alen house on the left. The Van Alen house is a restored Dutch farmhouse, furnished with 18th century Dutch furniture. It was built in 1737 by Luykas Van Alen although the marker indicates a year earlier. Van Alen was a wealthy farmer and merchant. The house is open to visitors, Thursday-Saturday from 11AM-5PM, Sunday from 1-5PM..

Mile Mark 117.0 — Watch for the Post Road marker on the right.

Birthsite

Martin Van Buren, eighth president of the United States, was born at this site December 5, 1782.

State Education
Department

(Kinderhook Marker)

Mile Mark 117.2 — Turn right off of Route 9H onto Route 21 going west to the town of Kinderhook.

Mile Mark 117.7 — Watch for the birthsite marker for Martin Van Buren on the left.

Mile Mark 118.0 — Arrive in the town of Kinderhook and the intersection with US Route 9. Park near the small park in the center of town and take a short walking tour of Kinderhook. Begin at the Knox Trail marker in the center of the park.

KINDERHOOK

Knox Trail — During the months of November, December and January, 1775-1776, Henry Knox led a transportation unit that brought artillery from Fort Ticonderoga and Crown Point for a siege of Boston. The 300-mile route taken by Knox is called the Knox Trail. Knox did not have the benefit of good roads or wagons for the trip. They used flat-bottom scows to cross Lake George, which were specially constructed sleds for snow, ice and frozen lakes. They completed the journey in trains pulled by horses and oxen. They transported 44 cannons, 14 mortars and one howitzer.

The Knox Trail marker has a map on it that shows the

Through this place passed Gen. Henry Knox in the winter of 1775-1776 to deliver to Gen. George Washington at Cambridge the train of artillery from Fort Ticonderoga used to force the British Army to evacuate Boston.

Erected by the State of New York during the Sesquicentennial of the American Revolution.

(Kinderhook Marker)

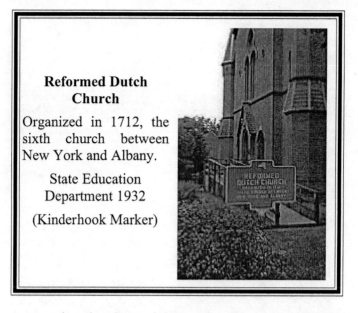

Reformed Dutch Church

Organized in 1712, the sixth church between New York and Albany.

State Education Department 1932

(Kinderhook Marker)

route taken by General Knox through New York. It includes Fort George, Fort Edward, Saratoga, Half-moon, Albany, Kinderhook, Claverack and Nobletown. Claverack is the turning point from south to east on the marker and is also close to the halfway point in the journey. The Claverack marker can be found on the Taconic Parkway. The Nobletown marker can be found on Route 22.

Reformed Dutch Church — A short walk south on the east side of US Route 9 brings you to the Reformed Dutch Church. The congregation, among the first in New York State, was formed in 1712.

Around the right side near the rear of the church is a memorial to Martin Van Buren.

Benedict Arnold House — About a tenth of a mile past the church and across the street is a small 18th century house with a Benedict Arnold marker in front. The marker is hard to see because it is almost

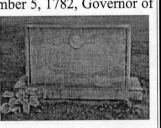
completely surrounded by trees. The marker identifies
the house as the Benedict Arnold House.

The battle that the marker refers to is the second battle
of Saratoga. It was during this battle that Benedict
Arnold was a true hero. Disobeying the orders of
General Horatio Gates and without any regard for his
own safety, he almost single-handedly rallied the
Americans to victory at Saratoga, a victory that is
recognized as the turning point in the American
Revolution. General John Burgoyne surrendered and
over 5,000 British soldiers became prisoners of war.

Benedict Arnold was, no doubt, a very complex person.
On Route 9D, at the beginning of this road trip, we saw

Benedict Arnold House

According to tradition,
Benedict Arnold was
brought here after being
wounded at the battle of
Bemis Heights, 1777.

Erected 1959

(Kinderhook Marker)

where Benedict Arnold took flight and became a traitor to the American cause. At the end of this road trip at Saratoga, we will see Benedict Arnold, a war hero — a true dichotomy.

Burgoyne House — A short walk back to the center of the town on the west side of US Route 9 brings you to a marker in front of a mansion home. This home was a stopping place for General John Burgoyne on his way to Boston. He was held here as both a prisoner and a guest.

Vanderpoel House — Not far from the "Burgoyne House" is the James Vanderpoel House. Vanderpoel was born shortly after the Revolution in 1787 and

General John Burgoyne

As prisoner of war, was entertained in this house on the night of October 22, 1777, while being taken from the Battle of Saratoga to Boston.

State Education Department

(Kinderhook Marker)

served the state of New York with distinction as a lawyer and judge. Today, the house is a fine example of Federal period architecture and is owned by the Columbia County Historical Society.

Columbia County Museum — A block west on Albany Street is the Columbia County Museum. It houses a research library, collections storage, and exhibit space. It is the current home of the Columbia County Historical Society.

Lunch in Kinderhook — Near the Vanderpoel House are a couple spots for lunch. Across the street is Bagel Tyme. They have great soups and bagel sandwiches. Just up the street from the Vanderpoel house is Valaggio's Pizzeria. Their pizza has won awards.

Mile Mark 118.0 — Back on US Route 9, leave Kinderhook heading north.

Mile Mark 118.8 — Reach the intersection with Route 9H, pass under Route 9H heading into the town of Valatie (pronounced val-é-sha).

Mile Mark 119.2 — Pass through the outskirts of the town of Valatie, circa 1665. Note the old Dutch architecture present in many of the homes.

Mile Mark 119.8 — Reach an intersection with Route 9H, bear right and continue going north on US Route 9. Just past the intersection on the right is a tavern marker.

Quackenboss Tavern

Here in 1753 for two months sat commissioners to divide the great Kinderhook patent of 1686. Martin Van Buren later tried a law case here.

State Education
Department

(US Route 9 Marker)

Mile Mark 121.1 — Look for the big apple floating overhead. What could be a more appropriate site in the heart of New York State? This is the home of the Golden Harvest Farms.

There are several opportunities to purchase apples along this section of US Route 9. Not to be missed is a cup of hot apple cider and a cider donut.

Mile Mark 124.8 — Reach the intersection with the Berkshire Spur of the New York Thruway. Pass under the bridge.

Mile Mark 125.3 — Reach the intersection with Interstate 90. Pass under the interstate.

Mile Mark 129.6 — Reach the intersection with US Route 20. At the center of the intersection is another Knox Trail marker. Turn left and continue heading north on US Route 9.

Mile Mark 130.5 — Reach another intersection with Interstate 90. Go over the interstate.

Mile Mark 130.9 — Watch for Old Post Road street sign

in the distance on the left and the Post Road marker on US Route 9, also on the left. This post road marker indicates six miles to Albany.

Mile Mark 132.7 — Pass the Greenbush Reformed Church on the left. There is a Knox Trail marker in front of the church.

Mile Mark 133.1 — Pass another post road marker on the left.

Mile Mark 136.0 — Note the distinctive Albany Skyline in the distance.

Mile Mark 136.3 — Watch for the Fort Crailo marker on the right.

Mile Mark 136.8 — When you see Eckert Drugs on the right, move over to the left lane and at the light, turn left onto Aiken Avenue. In the middle of this intersection is another Knox Trail marker, although this one might obscured by high brush.

Proceed down Aiken Avenue until it ends at an intersection with Broadway. Turn left on Broadway; Fort Crailo is a short distance on

Crailo

State Historic Site

(Rensselaer Marker)

the left. Pull into a parking spot on the right.

Mile Mark 137.0 — Fort Crailo is a distinctive, 18th century home overlooking the Hudson River. It is the legendary home of the patriotic song "Yankee Doodle," penned during the French and Indian War.

Today, Fort Crailo is museum that depicts early Dutch life in the upper Hudson River Valley. It is open for tours from Wednesday-Saturday from 10 a.m. to 5 p.m.

From the park across from Fort Crailo, you can see the Albany Harbor and the Port of Albany. Docked in the Albany Harbor is the Dutch Apple II, a small cruise ship that tours the Hudson near Albany. Also docked in the harbor is the USS Slater, a destroyer escort ship that did service during World War II that today is a floating museum.

From Fort Crailo, reverse direction on Broadway and proceed past Aiken Avenue and return back to US Route 9, turning left at the light.

Mile Mark 137.9 — Cross the Hudson River and get into the right lane, following Route 9 north. After crossing the bridge, head up the west side of the Hudson following US Route 9 north onto Clinton Avenue. When you reach the light on Broadway, note the Quackenbush House on the right. It is an old Dutch brick home in a small park on the right. Go through the first light at Broadway and then get into the left lane and turn left onto Pearl Street. Once on Pearl Street, try to find a parking place at a parking meter. If that is not successful, there is a parking garage up on the left.

Mile Mark 139.1 — Arrive in Albany.

ALBANY

Quackenbush House – In Quackenbush Square is the Quackenbush house and the Albany Visitor Center. The house is the former home of Hendrick Quackenbush, an officer who served in the Revolutionary War. After Saratoga, Quackenbush was

Quackenbush House

Circa 1730, the oldest existing structure in the city of Albany. The house is considered to be one of the finest remaining examples of Dutch urban architecture in this country. The original stepped front gable was modified to its present federal style when the house was expanded around 1790 by Colonel Hendrique Quackenbush, who inherited the home from his father. Colonel Quackenbush was the leader of Albany's 5th Military Regiment which fought against Burgoyne's army at Saratoga in 1777. The house remained connected to the Quackenbush-Lansing family until after the American Civil War.

(Albany Marker)

responsible for the prisoner, General John Burgoyne, and it is believed that he was a prisoner/guest at the house. Today, it is the oldest house in Albany and is currently the home of Nicole's Bistro, a very popular local restaurant.

Albany Visitor Center – Next to the Quackenbush House is the Albany Visitor Center. In the center are many exhibits that cover the history of Albany. They include many old drawings and maps of Albany from the Revolutionary War period as well as periods before and after. At the center, you can pick up a pamphlet entitled, "Capital City! A Walking Tour." The complete tour is recommended on a longer visit to the area.

The Tricentenial Park – Diagonally across the street from Quackenbush Square is Tricentenial Park. The park was built in 1986 and commemorates Albany's 300th anniversary from 1686.

First Church in Albany – Diagonally across from Tricentennial Park is First Church. Inside is the oldest pulpit and weathercock in America brought from the Church of Amsterdam in 1656. On top of the building is a replica of the weathercock, bullet holes and all.

Schuyler Mansion – The mansion is on the south side of Albany and can be reached by following Pearl Street across Madison Avenue, turning right on Morton Avenue just past the Department of Motor Vehicles, turning left at the tiny, Schuyler Mansion directional sign on Clinton Street and finally turning right at the base of the mansion onto Catherine Street. There is a parking lot behind the mansion.

Philip Schuyler's Revolutionary War home is a state historic site. The mansion is open Wednes-

Schuyler Mansion

Erected 1762. The home of Major General Philip Schuyler of the American Revolution. Patriot, soldier, statesman. 1733-1804.

(Albany Marker)

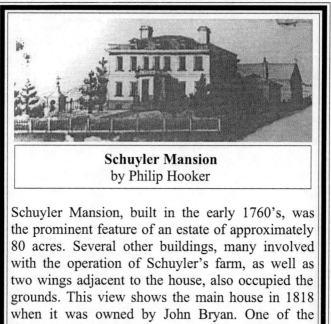

Schuyler Mansion
by Philip Hooker

Schuyler Mansion, built in the early 1760's, was the prominent feature of an estate of approximately 80 acres. Several other buildings, many involved with the operation of Schuyler's farm, as well as two wings adjacent to the house, also occupied the grounds. This view shows the main house in 1818 when it was owned by John Bryan. One of the wings and Schuyler's large Dutch barn appear at the right of the house. The vestibule on the front of the house was added after Schuyler's death in 1804.

(Albany Marker)

day-Saturday, 10AM-5PM, Sunday, 1-5PM. The small carriage house near the mansion is the Visitor Center. You are instructed to ring the bell for a tour.

There are two markers at the front of the house, one at the approach to the front door of the mansion and another at the top of the steps.

Burgoyne was also a prisoner/guest at the Schuyler Mansion. He stayed here with his 20-member staff for ten days before moving on to Boston. During that time, he and his staff enjoyed the hospitality of Philip Schuyler's wife, Catherine Van Rensselaer Schuyler.

In December 1780, the Marquis de Chastellux wrote: "A handsome house, halfway up the bank opposite the ferry, seems to attract the eye and to invite strangers to stop at General Schuyler's who is its owner as well as its architect. I had recommendations to him from all quarters, but particularly from General Washington and Mrs. Carter, Schuyler's daughter. On shore was the Chevalier de Mauduit, who was waiting for us with the General's sleigh and found ourselves in an instant in a handsome drawing room near a good fire with Mr. Schuyler, his wife and daughter. While we were warming ourselves, dinner was served to which everyone did honor as well as to the Madiera which was excellent and which made us completely forget the rigor of the season and the fatigue of the journey."

(Albany Marker)

Alexander Hamilton and the Schuylers' daughter, Elizabeth were engaged in March 1780. Their marriage took place at the mansion in December of the same year. After the marriage in July 1781, Hamilton served under Lafayette and participated in the siege at Yorktown.

Also in the summer of 1781, the Schuyler Mansion was attacked by a band of Tories. The attackers attempted to take Schuyler prisoner, but he was prepared for the attack and fought them off from his bedroom. To this day, there is a hatchet mark on the stairway banister that resulted from a thrown tomahawk during the attack.

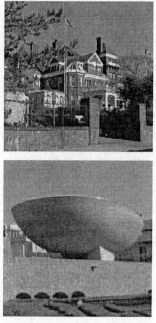

Fort Frederick – In 1777, Fort Frederick was target-center for Burgoyne's British invasion from Canada. The site of Fort Frederick can be reached by returning to Morton Avenue, taking Morton up to the light at Eagle Street, turning right on Eagle Street and following Eagle Street past the Governor's mansion, the Cathedral of the Immaculate Conception, the Corning Tower, the Egg (a sculpture that contains two back-to-back theatres) and the New York State Capitol Building. Short-term parking is available in front of City Hall, which is just past the capitol building on the right.

Facing the river on an eminence in this broad street, opposite St. Peter's Church stood Fort Frederick. Built about 1676, re-moved in 1784, Callows Hill to the south, fort burial ground to the north.

(Albany Marker)

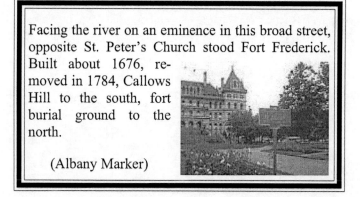

Fort Frederick
Albany Visitor Center Exhibit

In the middle of this street to the east stood Fort Frederick, goal of Burgoyne's drive to split the colonies in 1777.

(Albany Marker)

There are several markers on Eagle Street near the State Capitol. One of the markers is a ground marker near the road. Fort Frederick was built by the British in 1675.

City Hall – City Hall is at the intersection with Eagle Street. In front of City Hall is a statue of General Philip Schuyler. Although the statue depicts a stern, strong and triumphant Schuyler, it is often characterized as "brooding" — this, in reference to his failed invasion of Canada in 1776,

the loss of Fort Ticonderoga in 1777 and his replacement by General Horatio Gates as Commander of the Northern Department of the Continental Army prior to the battles of Saratoga.

Schuyler was later vindicated by Congress and should be remembered more for his ability in building and supplying the army's Northern Department. The British retreated twice from the army that he built, once at Fort Ticonderoga and Mount Independence in 1776 and again at Saratoga in 1777.

Just up the street from City Hall heading west is a highway marker. The marker highlights Albany's place as a crossroad. During the Revolution, military roads ran north, south, east and west from Albany. Today, interstates, US highways and railroads do the same as well as the waterways that run west, north and south.

The Kings Highway

First road to Schenectady began here near the west gate of the Albany Stockade.

(Albany Marker)

ALBANY TO SARATOGA BATTLEFIELD

Mile Mark 141.1 — Back in your car, proceed west on Washington Avenue, the old Kings Highway, which is Route 5 today.

Mile Mark 142.6 — Bear right at the split onto Central Avenue and take the next right onto Henry Johnson Boulevard.

Mile Mark 142.9 — Reach Clinton Avenue and the intersection with US Route 9. Cross the intersection and continue going north on Route 9.

Mile Mark 143.7 — Cross over Interstate 90 once again.

Mile Mark 145.4 — Pass through the town of Loudonville.

Mile Mark 146.2 — Pass Siena College on the right.

Mile Mark 148.2 — Crawl through the many traffic lights in the town of Latham.

Mile Mark 151.0 — Reach the intersection with Route 9R. Continue going straight.

Mile Mark 153.5 — As you approach the Mohawk River, watch for the Loudon Ferry Marker on the right. The marker indicates that Knox crossed the Mohawk here.

In the early 1800's, the Erie Canal also crossed the Mohawk River at this site. The aqueduct was a wooden structure supported by twelve stone piers. Today, US Route 9 crosses the Mohawk River and the Erie Canal, which are one and the same at this site.

Loudon Ferry Road

1755 — Constructed as a military road from Albany to Lake George by provincial troops from New York, New England and New Jersey under the command of Major General William Johnson.

Named in honor of Major General John Campbell, 4th Earl of Loudon. Commander in Chief of his Majesty's Forces in America. French and Indian War.

1776 — General Henry Knox's train of artillery crossed here to aid General George Washington in the siege of Boston.

Military Route Northern Department Continental Army.

1777 — Used as a camp ground of General Enoch Poor's Brigade.

Erected by New York State Education Department City of Cohoes, Cohoes Historical Society, 1938

(Cohoes Marker)

The marker also indicates that Enoch Poor's Brigade encamped in this area in 1777. Many American units camped in this area and the area ahead in preparation for the British invasion from Canada.

After crossing the bridge, turn right onto Terminal Road and pull into the parking area that is off on the right side of the bridge. Walk down to the water's edge and look west up the river under the US Route 9 bridge. In the distance is another bridge — the Thaddeus Kosciuszko Bridge on Interstate 87, the

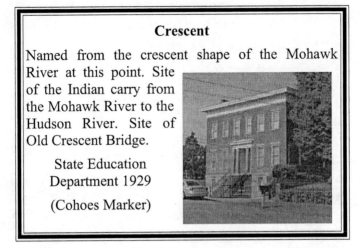

Crescent

Named from the crescent shape of the Mohawk River at this point. Site of the Indian carry from the Mohawk River to the Hudson River. Site of Old Crescent Bridge.

State Education Department 1929

(Cohoes Marker)

"Northway." The bridge, which is familiar to thousands of commuters everyday, is named in honor of the Polish General who engineered the American defensive positions at Saratoga and many other areas during the Revolution, including West Point.

Return back to US Route 9 heading north on the "Halfmoon Parkway." The town of Halfmoon is named after the ship that Henry Hudson sailed when he explored the Hudson River Valley in 1609.

Mile Mark 157.8 — As you pass through the town of Clifton Park, watch for the hotel marker on the right. The marker indicates that this intersection existed back in the late 1700's.

> ### Hotel, Circa 1790
>
> Stop on Plank Road Turnpike from Waterford to Jonesville and Ballston Spa. Served as court house, jail and dance hall.
>
> Clifton Park
> Bicentennial Committee
>
> (Clifton Park Marker)
>
>

Mile Mark 159.4 — Down to the right on old US Route 9 is the Olde Dublin Restaurant, which dates back to the end of the American Revolution.

Mile Mark 162.8 — Pass Round Lake on the right.

Mile Mark 165.4 — Proceed through the town of Malta. There is a marker indicating that Colonel Elmer Ellsworth was born here. Ellsworth was killed during the Civil War after removing a confederate flag from a hotel in Alexandria, VA on May 24, 1861, the day after Virginia seceded from the Union.

Mile Mark 167.1 — Detour right after the Ripe Tomato Restaurant onto Route 9P,

> ### Olde Dublin Restaurant
> Since 1782
>
> (Clifton Park Road Sign)
>
>

which goes around the east side of Saratoga Lake to the Saratoga Battlefield.

Mile Mark 167.9 — Pass the Wiggins-Brown-Nolen Vernacular Greek Revival Farmhouse, Circa 1840, on the left.

Mile Mark 168.8 — Watch for scenic views of Saratoga Lake on the left.

Mile Mark 171.1 — Reach the intersection with Route 423, bear right to the Saratoga Battlefield.

Mile Mark 173.2 — Watch for the site marker for the First Baptist Church on the left.

Mile Mark 174.0 — Reach the intersection with Route 32. Turn left onto the route heading north.

Mile Mark 176.2 — Turn right into the Saratoga National Battlefield. Watch for the sign to the Visitor Center and pull into the parking lot. Arrive at the Saratoga Battlefield.

Saratoga 2000

The site of the First Baptist Church. Founded in 1762 by a group from Rhode Island. Burial site of Elder Lemuel Powers, father of Abigail Fillmore.

Town & Village of Stillwater

(Stillwater Marker)

SARATOGA BATTLEFIELD

The Visitor Center is a museum, a gift shop and a theatre. The theatre plays a film that introduces visitors to the Battles of Saratoga. There is a one-way, toll road around the battlefield and you can purchase the $5 pass at the Visitor Center.

With the toll road pass, you will receive a pamphlet that can be used in conjunction with the maps and exhibits in the Visitor Center and the interpretive markers on the battlefield itself to help you understand the Battles of Saratoga. The complete tour, which begins at the south end of the parking area, covers over

So We May All Be FREE

Black Soldiers at Saratoga

"Serving in racially mixed units, the Negro did not stand out distinctly; his military personality blended into the composite portrait of the undistinguished but indispensable foot soldier."

Benjamin Quarles, The Negro in the American Revolution

The Continental Army was not a racially segregated one. The U.S. Army would not field racially mixed units again until the Korean Conflict. An official return noting the number of black soldiers in the army a little less than a year after Saratoga shows the brigades that served in that campaign to be about 4% black. Since most of those for whom records still exist enlisted in 1777 for 3 years, or the duration of the war, it may be safe to assume that a similar proportion existed during the Saratoga Campaign. Generally the black soldier in the Continental Army was a musket-carrying private. Some were free, some would earn freedom by their service, and some, having fought for American Independence, would remain slave. In 1819, some would receive Government pensions for their Revolutionary service. Records of these pensions include men such as Caesar Wallace, born in Africa, who served in the 2nd New Hampshire Regiment; Agrippe Hull, born free in Northampton, Massachusetts, who served as orderly for Col. Thaddeus Kosciuszko; Dan Woodman, also of the 2nd New Hampshire

(Continued on page 115)

(Continued from page 114)

Regiment, who fought in the Battles of Saratoga, Monmouth, and Newtown; and Cornelius Woodmore, a drummer in the 2nd New York Regiment. The New Hampshire and New York Regiments bore the brunt of the fighting in both Battles of Saratoga. Black soldiers were also listed among the casualties at Saratoga: Sampson Brown, of the 15th Massachusetts, wounded in the hip by cannonball; Peter Brewer, of the 1st New Hampshire, killed on October 7th, 1777.

The arming of blacks was a source of concern for officers, many of whom were slaveowners themselves. General Philip Schuyler and Horatio Gates owned slaves in 1777. Facing the threat of invasion from Canada by British Gen. Burgoyne, and a thrust against Philadelphia by Gen. Howe, the Americans found they needed as many men as possible for long term service in the Continental Army. The yeoman farmers who turned out as Minutemen found they could not neglect their harvests at will or their families would starve. With the call going out for recruits to enlist for 3 years or the duration of the War, younger men, those with little or no property, began to enlist, changing the character of the Army. With less to lose, they were attracted by enlistment bounties and promises of western land grants at the war's close. By their service they would buy into this new society they were helping to create. Some free blacks were attracted by such incentives. In many cases a slave

(Continued on page 116)

(Continued from page 115)

would serve in place of his master, though not all would win freedom as a result.

Gen. Schuyler commented on this changing character of the Army in a letter to Gen. Heath on July 28, 1777, "...of the few Continental troops we have had ... one-third part is composed of men too far advanced in years for field service; of boys, or rather children, and mortifying barely to mention, of Negroes."

Their treatment and assignments were not without prejudice. Maj. Ebeneezer Stevens noted in his orderly book shortly after the Battle of Saratoga, "The Majors of the Brigade are to furnish Col. Hay ... with sixty Negroes to be employed as a standing fatigue party ..."

Some men who served in the ranks with blacks found, to their apparent surprise, that their compatriots differed little from themselves. Henry Hallowell, a soldier in the 5th Massachusetts Regiment, wrote in his journal, "In our company was four Negroes named Jeptha Ward, Job Upton, Duglass Middleton and Pomp Simmons and part of them called on me after their time was out. They had been good solders."

This exhibit was produced by the National Park Service with funds donated by the visitors to Saratoga National Historical Park and from Eastern National Park and Monument Association. Mr. Charles F. Patterson, of Super Speed Printing, donated the typesetting.

(Visitor Center Exhibit)

To the Left — Breymann Redoubt — .5 Miles

Straight Ahead — Balcarres Redoubt — .75 Miles

To the Right — American Camp — 2 Miles

(Saratoga Marker)

nine miles and contains ten tour stops. Although the tour is set up primarily for automobiles, bicycles are also very popular. In addition, there are walking paths and trails for horses.

In the back of the Visitor Center is a directional sign marker and a 200th Anniversary marker.

The First Battle of Saratoga – On the 19th of September 1777, British Forces under the command of General Burgoyne advanced south in three separate columns upon the American Forces who had set up defenses here. Two of the columns moved through the forests covering the region just west of the Hudson

200th Anniversary, 1777-1977

Battles of Saratoga

These fields now echo the sounds of silence and peace thanks to the men who won American victory.

Placed by the Admiral George Brown Chapter of the Empire State Society Sons of the American Revolution.

(Saratoga Battlefield)

River. The third, composed of German troops, marched down the old military road along the river.

American scouts first detected Burgoyne's forces and notified General Gates, who ordered Colonel Daniel Morgan's Virginia riflemen to track the British advance. Shortly after 12 PM, some of Morgan's men made contact with the advance guard of the center column. The contact took place in a clearing known as the Freeman Farm, which is Tour Stop 1.

Freeman Farm Overlook

In 1777 this land was owned and farmed by John Freeman, a loyalist who went north and joined the British invasion force. The major fighting of September 19 took place in the fields in front of you. Morgan's Virginia riflemen opened the battle shortly before noon by firing on the advance guard of Burgoyne's center column from their post in the Freeman House.

(Saratoga Marker)

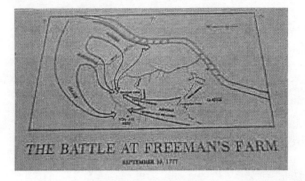

THE BATTLE AT FREEMAN'S FARM

SEPTEMBER 19, 1777

Tour Stop 1 – Freeman Farm. The battle that followed swayed back and forth over the farm for more than three hours. However, in the face of deadly fire from the numerically superior Americans, the British lines began to waver. But then German reinforcements arrived from the military road and attacked the American right, Burgoyne was able to steady the

---

1777 — 1927

"I dedicate this gun to the American cause," Colonel Joseph Cilley

In honor of Enoch Poor, Brigadier-general of the New Hampshire Troops, Joseph Cilley, Colonel of the First Regiment, Henry Dearborn, Colonel of the Second Regiment, Alexander Scammell, Colonel of the Third Regiment and the New Hampshire men who fought in these decisive battles.

Erected by the State of New Hampshire.

(Saratoga Battlefield

British lines and gradually force the Americans to withdraw back to the American camp near Neilson Farm, which is Tour Stop 2.

Just before the stop is a monument placed in memory of Thaddeus Kosciuszko. Thousands of commuters are very familiar with another tribute to this great war hero – The Thaddeus Kosciuszko Bridge across the Mohawk River on the Northway (Interstate 87).

Across from the Kosciuszko monument is an area set aside for the unknown soldiers of Saratoga. A memorial is located near several unmarked graves.

Tour Stop 2 – Neilson Farm. American staff officers used Neilson Farm for quarters. Near the farm is a line of white polls that mark American positions. Down the hill there is a line of blue polls that mark British positions.

On the 19th of September 1777, the timely arrival of the German troops and the near exhaustion of the American's ammunition

allowed Burgoyne to reach these positions. The British commander ordered his troops to entrench in the vicinity of the Freeman Farm and await support from British Forces under the command of General Clinton, who was supposedly preparing to move north toward Albany from New York City. For nearly three weeks he waited, but Clinton did not arrive.

Though he held the immediate field of battle, Burgoyne had been stopped north of the American line that stretched from Bemis Heights to the powerful river fortifications near the

Thaddeus Kosciuszko
by H. B. Hall

> ## Unknown Soldiers of
> ## the Battles of Saratoga
>
> The unknown American soldiers who perished in the battles of Saratoga, September 19 and October 7, 1777 and were here buried in unmarked graves helped to assure the triumph of the war of independence to create the Republic of the United States of America and to establish liberty throughout the world. In honor of these patriots and in recognition of the bicentennial of the birth of George Washington, this memorial is erected by the Daughters of the American Revolution in New York State, 1931.
>
> (Saratoga Marker)

Hudson River, which is Tour Stop 3.

Tour Stop 3 – River Fortifications. At this position, you can hear the traffic going by on US Route 4 below. You cannot see the road, but in 1777 the trees would have been cleared.

The Second Battle of Saratoga – By the 7th of October 1777, Burgoyne's situation was critical. Faced by a growing American army and no help from Clinton from the south, and supplies rapidly diminishing, the British army was becoming weaker with each

passing day. Burgoyne had to choose between advancing or retreating. He ordered a reconnaissance-in-force to test the American left flank. Ably led and supported by eight cannon, a force of 1,500 men moved out of the British camp. An American outpost on a ridge near Chatfield Farm, which is Tour Stop 4, spotted the British movement.

American River Fortifications

This powerful position was established under the direction of Col. Thaddeus Kosciuszko, a Polish military engineer and volunteer in the patriot cause, and it proved to be the key to American strategy against Burgoyne in 1777. Patriot infantry and cannon posted here, supported by batteries along the near riverbank, closed off the Hudson Valley route to Albany and forced the British to attack the main American line on Bemis Heights on September 19.

(Saratoga Marker)

Tour Stop 4 – Chatfield Farm. After marching southwesterly about three quarters of a mile, the troops deployed in a clearing on the Barber Farm, which is Tour Stop 5. Most of the British were positioned in an

Anchor of the American Line

Artillery and Infantry positions along this bluff commanded the road to Albany. This defense line forced the British to fight on American terms.

(Saratoga Marker)

If the Redcoats had advanced down the road below toward Albany, the guns of this strongpoint would have been the first to greet them. In 1777, the road swung from its present route diagonally across the field below you toward the river.

(Saratoga Marker)

open field, but both flanks rested in woods.

Tour Stop 5 – Barber Farm. The Americans knew that Burgoyne's army was again on the move and at about 3 PM attacked in three

Chatfield Farm

An American outpost on this ridge, the site of Asa Chatfield's farm in 1777, spotted the British movement toward the Barber Farm on October 7. Beyond the ridge before you is Middle Ravine, across which American and British pickets exchanged musket shots between the first and second battles.

(Saratoga Marker)

columns under Colonel Morgan, General Ebenezer Learned, and General Enoch Poor. Repeatedly, the British line was broken, then rallied. Both flanks were severely punished and driven back. General Simon Fraser, who commanded the British right, was mortally wounded as he rode among his men encouraging them to stand and cover the developing withdrawal.

Before the enemy's flanks could be rallied, General Benedict Arnold, who had been relieved of command

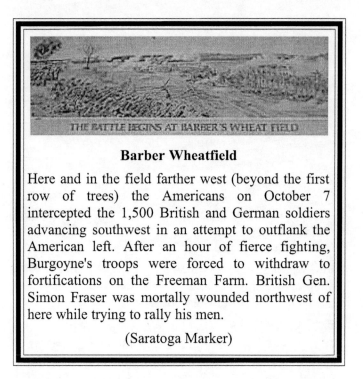

THE BATTLE BEGINS AT BARBER'S WHEAT FIELD

Barber Wheatfield

Here and in the field farther west (beyond the first row of trees) the Americans on October 7 intercepted the 1,500 British and German soldiers advancing southwest in an attempt to outflank the American left. After an hour of fierce fighting, Burgoyne's troops were forced to withdraw to fortifications on the Freeman Farm. British Gen. Simon Fraser was mortally wounded northwest of here while trying to rally his men.

(Saratoga Marker)

after a quarrel with Gates, rode onto the field and led Learned's brigade against the German troops holding the British center. Under tremendous pressure from all sides, the Germans joined a general withdrawal into the

Re-enactors Move into Position at Saratoga

fortifications on the Freeman Farm. Within an hour after the opening clash, Burgoyne lost eight cannon and more than 400 officers and men.

Flushed with success, the Americans believed that victory was near. Arnold led one column in a series of savage attacks on the Balcarres Redoubt, which is Tour Stop 6. The redoubt was a powerful British fieldwork on the Freeman Farm.

Tour Stop 6 – Balcarres Redoubt. After repeated American failures to carry Balcarres Redoubt, General Benedict Arnold wheeled his horse and dashed through

Balcarres Redoubt

(Freeman Farm)

Balcarres Redoubt was a log-and-earthen work about 500 yards long and 12 to 14 feet high. Named for Lord Balcarres, who commanded the British light infantry, it formed the strongest part of the fortified line constructed between the Hudson River and the Breymann Redoubt by Burgoyne's troops after the battle of September 19. On October 7 the British flanking column withdrew here after being driven from the Barber Farm. The redoubt is outlined by posts.

(Saratoga Marker)

the crossfire of both armies to the Breymann Redoubt, which is Tour Stop 7. Arnold arrived just as American troops began their assault on British fortifications. He joined in the final surge that overwhelmed the German soldiers defending the work. Upon entering the redoubt, he was wounded in the leg. Had he died

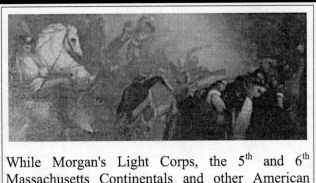

While Morgan's Light Corps, the 5th and 6th Massachusetts Continentals and other American troops, attacked the Breymann Redoubt from the front, the intrepid Benedict Arnold without a command of his own joined a handful of Americans on a daring assault from the rear. Near this spot, Arnold was shot in the leg. The nameless boot monument symbolizes his bravery as well as his subsequent treason.

(Saratoga Marker)

during this assault, there is no doubt that posterity would have known few names more heroic than that of General Benedict Arnold.

Tour Stop 7 – Breymann Redoubt. Darkness ended the day's fighting and saved Burgoyne's army from immediate defeat. That night the British commander

Breymann Redoubt

Breymann Redoubt, also outlined by posts, was a single line of breastworks about 200 yards long and 7 to 8 feet high. It guarded the British right flank and the road to Quaker Springs. It was named for Lt. Col. Heinrich Breymann, whose German troops were stationed here.

(Saratoga Marker)

left his campfires burning, abandoned British Headquarters, which is Tour Stop 8, and began pulling his forces back to the North.

Failing to capture Balcarres Redoubt, the Americans surged against Crown Forces fortifications built here called the Breymann Redoubt. Attacking relentlessly they overwhelmed this important defensive position just before nightfall, October 7, 1777. Never more than a crude barrier of logs, this fortification is now known as the Breymann Redoubt, named after the German officer who commanded the German Grenadier defenders.

(Saratoga Marker)

Tour Stop 8 – British Headquarters. Burgoyne withdrew his troops behind the Great Redoubt that protected the high ground and river flats at the northeast corner of the battlefield.

After you leave Tour Stop 8, you will cross a high bridge over a stream and the entrance road that, at this point, parallels the stream. The high ground that you are traveling to is the Great Redoubt and includes Tour Stops 9 and 10.

Tour Stop 9 – Great Redoubt. From the top of the redoubt, there is a view of the entrance to the park on US Route 4 and the Hudson River in the distance. Picnic tables make it a great spot for an afternoon picnic or just a place to sit and contemplate the events of 1777.

Benedict Arnold
by H. B. Hall

BURGOYNE'S HEADQUARTERS

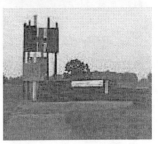

Burgoyne's Headquarters

The path here leads to the site of Burgoyne's headquarters, which at the time of the battles consisted of a large marquee or tent. It was established after the action of September 19 and was the center of British command and camp life between the two battles. Burgoyne chose the location because of a nearby spring.

(Saratoga Marker)

On the night of the 8th of October 1777, the British buried General Fraser and began a hasty retreat northward. They had suffered about 1,000 casualties in the fighting of the past three weeks; American losses numbered

The Great Redoubt

The Great Redoubt was a system of fortifications built by the British on this hill and two others to the north. It was designed to guard their hospital, artillery park, and supplies on the river flat, and the boat bridge across the Hudson. Burgoyne withdrew his army to this vicinity during the night of October 7.

(Saratoga Marker)

> The capture of the Breymann Redoubt forced Burgoyne to withdraw his army to a position centered on three fortifications. This is the second of these three fortifications that were referred to by the British as the Great Redoubt. They were built sometime between September 19th and October 7th, 1777.
>
> (Saratoga Marker)

less than 500. Saratoga was one of the most decisive victories in American and world history. It helped to convince the French to join the American cause, making it the turning point of the American Revolution.

Tour Stop 10 – Walking Trail. This tour stop commemorates the burial place of General Fraser and the British retreat. The tour stop is actually a walking

BURIAL SITE OF GENERAL FRASER

Fraser Burial Site and Trail

The British general, Simon Fraser, mortally wounded during the battle of October 7, 1777 was buried near this site the following day.

(Saratoga Marker)

trail that begins with a warning marker.

THE RIVER REDOUBTS

Beyond the gravesite, the trail goes to another site on the Great Redoubt. It continues down a steep hill between two fortifications and at the base of the hill, you reach an intersection at the base of the Great Redoubt. There is no indicator which direction to go, but if you take the trail to right, you will reach a marker for the British Hospital.

WARNING

Steep Grade

8/10ths of a Mile in Length

No Wheelchairs

(Saratoga Marker)

Reversing direction, you will pass several markers, including a marker for the artillery park and another for the extensive baggage carried by the British forces.

Main Crown Forces Hospital

Burgoyne's retreating army was forced to leave its sick and wounded to the care of the Americans. The main British medical facilities were located on the flat below to your right.

(Saratoga Marker)

Crown Forces Artillery Park

When Burgoyne ordered his army into retreat, the British force's artillery park located on the flat area below and to your right became a scene of frantic activity. The artillery equipment assembled here, larger field guns, spare carriages, carts for ammunition and tools, supply wagons, and even carriages for pontoons used to build floating bridges, all had to be hitched to oxen or horse and brought into line.

(Saratoga Marker)

Further down the trail is another intersection. Bearing to the right, you will cross a bridge that is near a surviving portion of the Old Champlain Canal built in the 1820's. Out, in a swampy field, one can see four

Crown Forces Baggage Park

When the order came to retreat, the civilian teamsters contracted by the British, many from Canada, began harnessing teams of horses and yoking pairs of oxen in the baggage park on the flat directly below you. Wagons and two wheeled carts, not already loaded, were hurriedly piled with officer's bedding, trunks and beds, pots and pans, barrels, and sacks of foodstuffs.

(Saratoga Marker)

SURVIVING PORTION OF CHAMPLAIN CANAL

posts which mark the corners of Taylor Cabin, where Simon Fraser died.

At this point, you may become aware of how deeply you have traveled into the marshy woods. Don't be surprised if you hear the sounds of creatures lurking about.

Reversing direction once again and bearing right at the intersection, you will return back to the parking lot, but not after a healthy climb up

---

Site of the Taylor Cabin

A grievously wounded Simon Fraser was carried here to the Taylor Cabin, which had been taken over as a residence by Baroness Riedesel, the wife of the German commander. The bleeding General was brought into the room where a cheerful dinner party to which he had been invited was being held. Simon Fraser died at 8:00 on the morning of October 8, 1777.

(Saratoga Marker)

138

The Great Redoubt
by Barlow

a steep hill. There are benches on the way where you can rest during the climb.

Back in the car, the tour ends at an intersection with the entrance road. Total mileage in the park is about 12 miles.

Baroness Riedesel
by Tischbein

SARATOGA BATTLEFIELD TO SCHUYLERVILLE

Mile Mark 185.7 — At the end of the battlefield toll road, turn left and depart the battlefield.

Mile Mark 186.0 — Reach the intersection with US Route 4. Turn left, heading north. Note that this river road is targeted by British artillery up on the hill to

Dovegat House

Headquarters, General Burgoyne during the advance and retreat of the British Army.

(US Route 4 Marker)

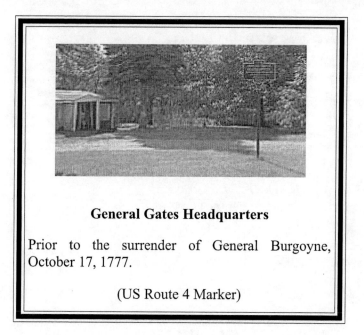

General Gates Headquarters

Prior to the surrender of General Burgoyne, October 17, 1777.

(US Route 4 Marker)

your left. These were the British redoubts visited at stops 9 and 10. Also, watch for nice views of the Hudson River on the right.

Mile Mark 190.5 — In front of a farm on the right is the Dovegat House marker.

Mile Mark 191.6 — In front of two homes on the right, there is a Gates Headquarters marker. If you pull

Here, General Burgoyne surrendered his sword to General Gates, Oct. 17, 1777.

(US Route 4 Marker)

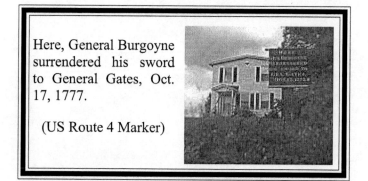

over for a closer look at the marker, watch out for the dogs.

Mile Mark 192.4 — Watch for the intersection with Schuyler Street on the right. Note the surrender marker on the hill.

Mile Mark 192.9 — Bear right into the country home of Philip Schuyler. Arrive in Schuylerville.

Surrender of General Burgoyne
by John Trumbull

SCHUYLERVILLE

In the months prior to October 8, 1777, the British suffered about 2,000 casualties. Burgoyne's forces, now down to about 6,000 men, took refuge in a fortified camp on the heights of Saratoga (today's Schuylerville). There an American force that was approaching 20,000 men surrounded the exhausted British army.

Faced with such overwhelming numbers, Burgoyne surrendered on October 17, 1777. By the terms of the Convention of Saratoga, Burgoyne's depleted army marched out of camp "with the Honors of War" and stacked their weapons along the west bank of the Hudson River at Fort Hardy.

Saratoga was a decisive and important victory. It was the turning point of the American Revolution.

Schuyler House – To see the many historical sites around Schuylerville, a loop around town is recommended. The first site is the Schuyler House.

Schuyler House

"We passed Hudson's River and encamped in the plains of Saratoga at which place there is a handsome and commodious dwelling house," so wrote an officer of British General John Burgoyne's invading army in September 1777. The dwelling house was the country home of wealthy landowner, Philip Schuyler. Less than a month later, his army reeling in defeat, Burgoyne ordered the house burned so the Americans could not use it for cover. Despite this precaution, the proud Burgoyne was forced to surrender his army on October 17, 1777 in a field not far from the smoldering ruins. Within weeks, Schuyler was earnestly engaged in building a house at this place. By the end of November 1777, the present building was completed, possibly built in part on the foundation of the old dwelling house. The present Schuyler House has been carefully restored to its 1787-1804 appearance.

(Schuylerville Marker)

November 28, 1745, on these grounds the French and Indians killed Captain Philip Schuyler and thirty others, burning mills, stores and thirty houses.

On June 30, 1747, the garrison of Fort Saratoga was surprised when 45 men were tomahawked and scalped.

Site of the house of Captain Schuyler, 1745 and General Philip Schuyler, 1777.

(Schuylerville Marker)

In front of the Schuyler house, there is a marker at the pathway entrance that relates its history. Depending on the time of the year, volunteers in period costume may be on hand to give you a tour of the house. Tours are scheduled on the half-hour.

Here in 1880 while excavating for the Bullard Paper Mill, the remains of an unknown soldier and his horse were exhumed.

(Schuylerville Marker)

Near this spot, October 16, 1777, American and British officers met and consummated "Articles of Convention" of General Burgoyne of the British army to General Gates of the American army and on this historic ground of Saratoga the British army laid down its arms, October 17, 1777 thus assuring American independence.

(Schuylerville Marker)

Across from the house on US Route 4 is a Schuyler Marker. The marker shows the sacrifice made by the Schuyler family to colonize this area.

Revolutionary War Markers in Schuylerville – Returning back to US Route 4, there are two markers on the right just after the bridge across the Fishkill River. One of the two is a Knox Trail marker. The other is about the recovery of a soldier and a horse.

There is also a Conventions of Saratoga marker on the right across from Burgoyne Avenue.

Saratoga Monument

The Saratoga Monument commemorates the surrender of the British Army under the command of General John Burgoyne to General Horatio Gates commander of the America forces on 17 October 1777 following the battles of Saratoga. The battles and subsequent surrender are considered a turning point in the American Revolution by leading to French support and the hope of ultimate victory. This lofty sight was chosen for the monument because of its commanding view of the surrounding battlefield sites and its historical association with Burgoyne's campaign. The cornerstone was laid on 17 October 1877, one hundred years after the British surrender. The capstone was put into place in 1882 and the decorative elements of bronze statues and interior bass relief was finally completed in 1887. A cast iron stairway lead up 184 steps to an observation deck which is closed.

(Schuylerville Marker)

Saratoga Monument – The monument is up Burgoyne Avenue, also County Route 338.

The monument commemorates the surrender of British Forces to American Forces on October 17, 1777. As explained by the marker in front of the monument, each side of the monument has a niche for each of the major American contributors in the Battles of Saratoga: Philip Schuyler, Daniel Morgan, Horatio Gates and Benedict Arnold.

The monument was refurbished in 2002 for the

Saratoga Monument

The three statues on the outside niches are bronze presentations of the major American players in the Battles of Saratoga. General Philip Schuyler, commander of the American forces during the greater part of the British invasion faces east toward his home. General Horatio Gates faces north. General Daniel Morgan, commander of the riflemen, faces west. The vacant niche facing south is in recognition of the leadership of Benedict Arnold who in 1780 turned traitor to the American cause.

(Schuylerville Marker)

225th Anniversary of the British surrender. Before refurbishing, one could not help but notice a little tree growing in the vacant niche where the statue of Benedict Arnold would have been. One wondered if Arnold was building his own statue from the grave.

A climb to the top of the monument is recommended for the non-acrophobic.

Revolutionary War Markers on the North Side of Schuylerville – Continuing past the Saratoga Monument and bearing right at the next several intersections, you will pass an old graveyard and several markers.

The first marker is at the position that Daniel Morgan and his riflemen took to stop a possible British retreat to the west. The marker is near a small cemetery where

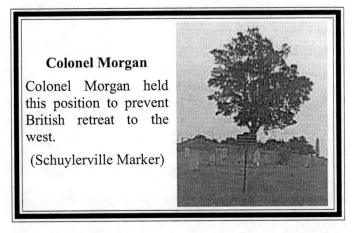

Colonel Morgan

Colonel Morgan held this position to prevent British retreat to the west.

(Schuylerville Marker)

many of the graves date back to the middle 1800's. Just past the cemetery at an intersection with Route 29 is a marker about the town of Saratoga.

A series of four markers can be found along Route 29 on the return back to US Route 4. There are two British encampment markers on the left. One is near a gift shop. The other is in front of a home near the Schuylerville Central School. There is a breastworks marker on the right opposite the school and there is a

Campground of the British Army

October 15, 1777.

(Schuylerville Marker)

> ## Continental Barracks
>
> Where General Stark tried and condemned the Tory, Lovelass as a spy.
>
> Camp of General Burgoyne
>
> October 10-17, 1777.
>
> (Schuylerville Marker)

barracks marker on the left, just before the intersection with US Route 4.

Fort Hardy Park – The park can be reached by turning right on US Route 4 south, turning left onto Broadway and crossing the old Champlain Canal and Tow Path.

The park is the site where the British laid down their arms after the battles of Saratoga. Today, Fort Hardy is an athletic park with soccer fields and other athletic facilities. Keeping the history alive on the west side of

On these fields, the British Army grounded arms at the surrender.

(Schuylerville Marker)

the field is the Schuylerville Visitor Center. Inside, there are history exhibits as well as information about Schuylerville. Near the visitor center is a marker for the Surrender Tree, under which the surrender documents were signed. There is also a surrender marker near the entrance to the park.

The Surrender Tree

The tree commemorates a great elm tree, under which it is said, the British General John Burgoyne signed the Convention of Saratoga by which he surrendered his forces to American General Horatio Gates, October 17, 1777. Considered to be the turning point of the American Revolution.

(Schuylerville Marker)

Town of Saratoga

Mother town of Saratoga County. First European settlers, 1688. Established, March 7, 1788. Surrender sight of General Burgoyne to General Gates, October 17, 1777.

(Schuylerville Marker)

SCHUYLERVILLE TO SARATOGA SPRINGS

Mile Mark 195.7 — From the Visitor Center, drive to Ferry Street and turn right just before the Post Office. Cross the bridge over the old Champlain Canal and turn right onto Route 29 west.

Mile Mark 196.1 — Reach a light at an intersection with US Route 4. Turn left and continue west on Route 29. This section of Route 29 is called the "General Schuyler Commemorative Highway."

Mile Mark 196.6 — Watch for views of the Saratoga Monument on the left.

Mile Mark 200.8 — Pass Wind Hill Farm. With two famous racetracks in Saratoga Springs, horses are big in this area.

Mile Mark 204.9 — Go under Interstate 87.

Mile Mark 206.1 — Reach the light at East Street. Continue going straight on Lake Avenue.

Mile Mark 206.6 — Watch for the Armory — a castle-like building on the right. Today, it is a military museum. Go to the light and turn right onto Maple Avenue.

Mile Mark 207.1 — Park near the intersection of Rock Street and Maple Avenue. Arrive at the Bryan Home in Saratoga Springs.

SARATOGA SPRINGS

High Rock Spring — The intersection of Rock Street and Maple Avenue is where High Rock Spring is located. The spring has attracted people to this area for centuries. There are two markers in the area. One is at the Olde Bryan Inn. The other is down at the base of the rock near the spring buildings.

Legend has it that Indians visited the springs as early as 1300. They believed that the spring had medicinal properties and helped one gain strength. They called it the "Medicine Spring of the Great Spirit."

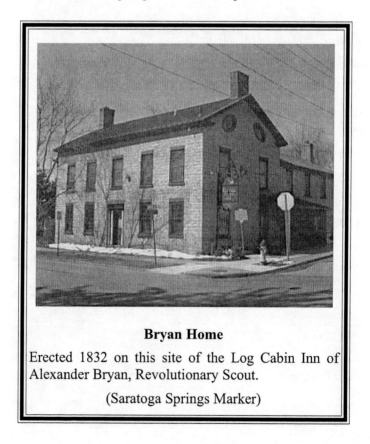

Bryan Home

Erected 1832 on this site of the Log Cabin Inn of Alexander Bryan, Revolutionary Scout.

(Saratoga Springs Marker)

The reputation of the spring grew tremendously during the French and Indian War. After Sir William Johnson was wounded at the Battle of Lake George, he was carried to the spring by Mohawk Indians. He was fed water from the spring and his health improved markedly. He was able to make parts of the return trip on his feet — a miracle attributed to the spring.

Saratoga's First Resort for Travelers

Called by the Mohawk Indians, "The Medicine Spring of the Great Spirit" now known as the High Rock Spring.

The first white man to visit the spring was Sir William Johnson in 1767.

General George Washington, Governor George Clinton and Alexander Hamilton visited General Philip Schuler here in 1783.

Erected by Bemis Heights Society of the Daughters of the American Revolution.

(Saratoga Springs Marker)

In 1774, the first inn for visitors opened at the spring. In 1777, the Norton family purchased the inn and operated it for over ten years, except for a brief interruption caused by the British invasion from Canada.

As the Revolutionary War came to a close, Philip Schuyler built a plank road from his summer home in Schuylerville to the springs. In 1783, George Washington came to Saratoga to inspect the battlefield and other fortifications in the area. Schuyler brought him to the High Rock Spring along with Alexander Hamilton and Governor Clinton. Washington was so impressed by the spring that he later attempted to purchase land in the area. His attempt was blocked by titles secured by Livingston and Walton.

After the Revolutionary War, the inn was purchased by Alexander Bryan. Bryan was an American spy during the Revolutionary War. Prior to the battles at Saratoga,

George Washington and Philip Schuyler

(Visitor Center Exhibits)

The Governor

This spring was drilled in 1908. It was named for Governor Charles Evans Hughes, who had recently signed a bill protecting the springs. The water flows through limestone and clay from a depth of 170 feet. The water also is piped over to the High Rock cone under the pavilion to your right.

The Peerless

This spring is located across High Rock Avenue and is piped to this fountain. It is very palatable with only a moderate amount of minerals.

Dept. of Public Works

(Saratoga Springs Marker)

Bryan entered Burgoyne's camp in an attempt to figure out the route of the British army. After learning of the British plan, his presence was discovered and he narrowly escaped. He reported his findings to General Gates and the information helped to secure the American victory.

Dinner in Saratoga Springs — Today, the Olde Bryan Inn, at the corner of Maple Avenue and Rock Street, is the restored inn once operated by Alexander Bryan. The inn is a popular eating establishment in Saratoga Springs and is a recommended spot for dinner.

The inn doesn't take reservations and you'll likely get put on a waiting list for a table. While you're waiting, take a walk down the stairway on the "High Rock." At the bottom of the stairway are two buildings to which spring water is piped. Water flows from several fountains inside one of the buildings. Taste the water from these "medicine springs."

Congress Park and the Visitor Center — If it's not too late in your **Revolutionary Day**, a walk around Congress Park is recommended. The park is about a mile drive south of the Old Bryan Inn on US Route 9. Route 9 is a block west of the inn.

As you enter the park, you'll pass a memorial on the left to Ellen Hardin Walworth, one of the founders of the Daughters of the American Revolution. On the right is

the Congress Spring, discovered in 1792 by Congressman John Gilman. The spring was later exploited by lumberman and entrepreneur, Gideon Putnam. In 1802, he built a hotel called Union Hall. By 1806, visitors were so numerous, a second hotel was built called Congress Hall. In the late 1800's, a casino was built. Today, the Casino is a museum and the current home of the Historical Society.

Across from Congress Park is the Visitor Center. The center has several exhibits about the history of Saratoga Springs and the attractions in the area.

Overnight in Saratoga Springs — A great place to stay is about a mile further south on US Route 9 in the Saratoga Springs State Park. The Gideon Putnam Hotel is a brick, Georgian style structure erected in 1935 and is located in the state park. Inside the park are several working springs and a geyser, spouting Saratoga's famous mineral water. Reservations are a must (518-584-3000).

BIBLIOGRAPHY

Albany Urban Center Park Visitor Center, "Capital City! A Walking Tour," 2002.

Bobrick, Benson, **Angel in the Whirlwind,** Penguin Books, New York, 1997.

Connolly, Courtney, Eileen Forrester and Jennifer Fragleasso, "Out & About," **Hudson Valley,** Volume XXIX, Number 1, Suburban Publishing, Poughkeepsie, NY 2000.

Deary, William P. PhD, "Defending the Lower Hudson River in 1776," **Sea History**, No. 98, National Maritime Historical Society, 2001.

Gold, Nancy Dana, "Victory, by George," **Hudson Valley**, Volume XXVIII, No. 10, Suburban Publishing, Poughkeepsie, NY, 2000.

Hamilton, Edward P., **Fort Ticonderoga, Key to a Continent,** Little, Brown and Company, Boston, 1964.

Johnson, Dr. James M., "A Warm Reception in the Hudson Highlands," **Sea History**, No. 98, National Maritime Historical Society, 2001.

Keller, Allan, **Life Along the Hudson,** Lake Champlain Publishing Company, Burlington, VT, 1997.

Clare O'Neill Carr, **A Brief History of Red Hook**, Wise Family Trust, New York, NY, 2001

Kelly, Nancy V., **A Brief History of Rhinebeck**, Wise Family Trust, New York, NY, 2001

Leonard, Roger M., **The Red Church,** Roger M. Leonard, Red Hook, NY, 1990.

Mid-Hudson Historic Consortium, "Historic Treasure of the Mid-Hudson Valley," Glenham, NY, 2001.

Mintz, Max M., **The Generals of Saratoga, John Burgoyne and Horatio Gates,** Yale University Press, New Haven, 1990.

Mount Gulian Historic Site, "The Verplanck Homestead, Birthplace of the Society of the Cincinnati, General von Steuben's Revolutionary War Headquarters," 1995.

National Park Service, US Department of the Interior, "Saratoga", GPO:1997—417-648/60107, 1997.

Office of Parks, Recreation and Historic Preservation, State of New York, "Clermont State Historic Site", 2001.

Office of Parks, Recreation and Historic Preservation, State of New York, "Schuyler Mansion", 1991.

Olde Bryan Inn, "Bryan Inn and High Rock Spring 1787," 2002.

Purcell, L. Edward and David F. Burg, Editors, **The World Almanac of the American Revolution,** Pharos Books, New York, 1992.

Stokes, Jennifer, "All's OK in Kinderhook," **Hudson Valley,** Volume XXX, Number 10, Suburban Publishing, Poughkeepsie, NY 2001.

Raymond C. Houghton is a freelance historian and sole proprietor of Cyber Haus of Delmar, NY. He is a retired college professor, former government bureaucrat, Vietnam Veteran and one-time, General Electric employee. He has honors from the Department of Commerce, is listed in Who's Who in America and holds a doctorate from Duke University.